POCKET HANDBOOK OF THE RUSSIAN FAR EAST:
A Reference Guide

Editors
Elisa Miller and Alexander Karp

Maps, design, and layout
Marilyn Milberger

Assistants to the Editors:
Jay Tettenhorst
Deborah Turnbull

Special thanks to
Institute of Economic Research
Far Eastern Branch
Russian Academy of Sciences (Khabarovsk)

**Pocket Handbook to the
Russian Far East:
A Reference Guide**

First edition: May 1994

Copyright © by *Russian Far East Update*
Box 22126, Seattle WA 98122
Telephone 206-447-2668
Telefax 206-628-0979
Elisa B. Miller, Editor and Publisher

ISBN# 0-9641286-0-8

P R E F A C E

Dear Reader—

When we were creating this pocket handbook of the Russian Far East, our goal was simple. We wanted to provide the reader with a "feel" for the Russian Far East. A feel for its space, its history, its resources.

Space: The Russian Far East is a very large place. It is two-thirds the size of the continental USA. Space and geography are important, and so we show you maps for each of the individual territories: maps which indicate the sparsity of the major cities and the limits of the region's infrastructure.

History: The Russian Far East is an arena where the interaction of several cultures and nations has created a particular historical dynamic. Wedged between China, Korea, Japan and the United States, Russian Far East history reflects aspirations of all these countries in the region. We bring you the details in an essay especially written for this volume by the West's leading scholar on the subject.

Resources: The Russian Far East is a treasure chest of natural resources: especially minerals, timber, fish. These resources mean interest in extraction, development, processing. It means business — involving the foreigner and the Russian entrepreneur. For this reason a major section of our book is devoted to a full understanding of the region's economy: its activities, its trade, its structure.

Business means travel, and a knowledge of how things work. We've included some practical advice: an essay on law, facts about telecommunications, lodging and travel, who's who.

The Russian Far East is a complicated place. We've tried to simplify where possible by anglicizing names of places. Thus instead of Khabarovskii Krai we simply say Khabarovsk. Instead of Primorskii Krai we say Primorye.

Finally, the Russian Far East is a changing place. For that reason we caution that our descriptions are good only to the date that we print them. Street names change, names of enterprises change, telephone numbers change. The economic system — whether it moves forward or backward — is also in a state of change. Our handbook captures the state of the region in transition. For the latest, up-to-date, information on any of the topics in this book, we refer you to our monthly publication, ***Russian Far East Update.***

The Editors

TABLE OF CONTENTS

LIST OF TABLES AND DIAGRAMS

East Siberian Sea

Laptev Sea

km 0   320   640

miles 0   200   400

Chukotskaia AO

Anadyr

Pacific Ocean

Koryakskii AOk

Republic of Sakha (Yakutiia)

Magadanskaia Oblast

Yakutsk

Magadan

Kamchatskaia Oblast

Petropavlovsk-Kamchatski

Sea Of Okhotsk

East Siberia

Kurile Islands

Sakhalinskaia Oblast

Amurskaia Oblast

Khabarovskii Krai

Yuzhno-Sakhalinsk

Buriatiia Republic

Lake Baikal

Chitinskaia Oblast

Blagoveshchensk

Khabarovsk

Ulan-Ude

Chita

Yevreyskaia (Jewish) AO

Aginskii-Buriatskii AOk

Mongolia

People's Republic of China

Primorskii Krai

Vladivostok

Japan

North Korea

Administrative Capital

AOk Autonomous Okrug

AO Autonomous Oblast

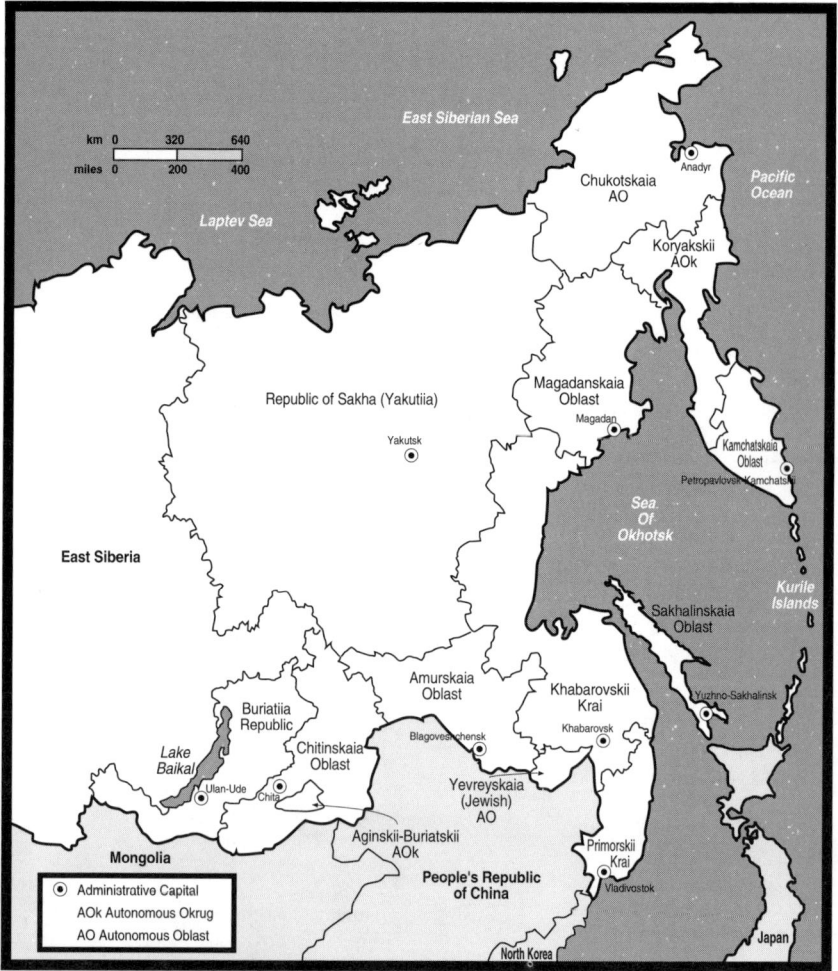

The Russian Far East:
Administrative Regions

Copyright © 1994 by Russian Far East Update
Seattle, Washington, USA

CHAPTER 1: TERRITORIAL SURVEY

The Region as a Whole

Political Structure

The Russian Far East is a group of nine territories, all of which have equal political stature under the jurisdiction of Russia (except for the Republic of Sakha which has greater autonomy). Two of these entities, Jewish Autonomous Oblast and Chukotka Autonomous Okrug, reached this status in the last few years. The Russian Far East has no formal political authority. It is simply an economic grouping of territories which encompasses the easternmost lands of Russia.

The region has attempted to form a political organization to represent its interests, the *Association of Far Eastern and Trans-Baikal Territories*, but conflict between the separate territories has meant limited success.

Diagram 1

Relative Level of Development of Russian Far East Territories

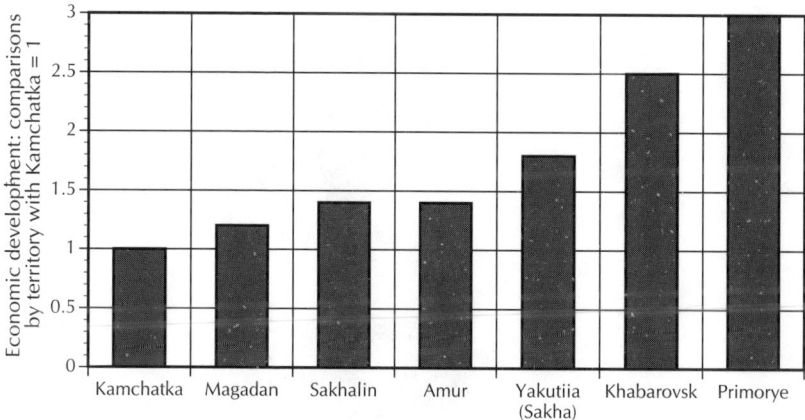

Data are for 1992.
The Russian Far East has two leading, relatively diversified, territories (Primorye and Khabarovsk); the other territories are smaller and more narrowly specialized.

Each territory is currently governed by the Head of the Administration (sometimes called the "governor") appointed by the President of the Russian Federation. Legislative bodies are also represented in each territory: formerly called the Territorial Council of Peoples Deputies, they are now called the local duma (parliament).

Economy

The Russian Far East is one of the least developed regions in Russia. It produces only 5% of Russia's national product and depends primarily on resource extraction. Its three major natural resources are marine biological resources, nonferrous metals, and timber.

The region produces almost all of the diamonds and tin of Russia and more than half of its gold and fish products. At the same time the region must import almost all of its oil, a substantial part of its coal, and one-half of its foodstuffs.

Diagram 2

Industrial Output in the Russian Far East: by Territory

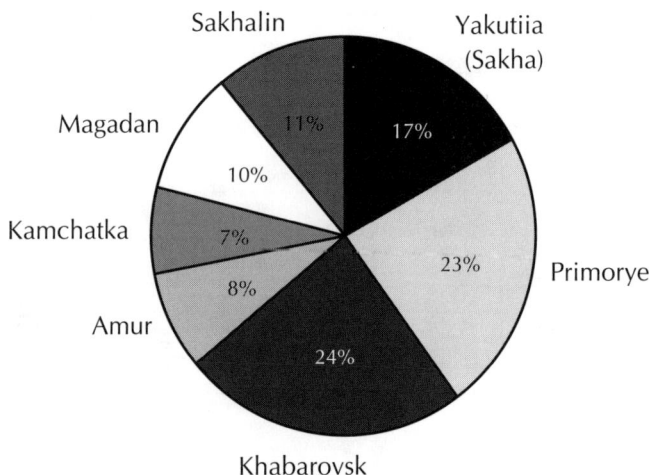

Sakhalin

Yakutiia (Sakha)

Magadan   11%   17%

10%

Kamchatka   7%

                    23%   Primorye

          8%

Amur

          24%

Khabarovsk

Data are for 1991.

Secondary to the extractive sectors—less understood, but still very significant—is manufacturing: machine building, defense production (nuclear submarines and ships), ship repair.

Basic Infrastructure

Transportation infrastructure in the Russian Far East is determined by the region's severe climate. Air transport is vital, especially in the region's North. The bulk of railways lie in the southern portion of the Russian Far East. Permafrost limits the construction of roads in the North. Rivers and coastal waterways remain important means of transport, although navigation is limited to months of the year when waters are ice free. Ice roads are a mode of transportation in the winter months.

Deficiencies are significant. For example, there is no automobile bridge across the Amur River linking Khabarovsk with the west bank of the river. The single railroad bridge needs modernization. Bottlenecks in the railroad-seaport intermodal link continue to present a barrier to increases in international trade flows. We mention the need for flood-control measures (in the South) as part of a plan for rational land use.

Geography

First, the region we are talking about is large: 2/3 the size of all the United States. Khabarovskii territory alone is 1.5 times the size of France. Second, and most notable, is the region's distance from Moscow (between Moscow and Vladivostok is 9216 km or 5620 miles), and its proximity to Pacific Rim nations. The region shares a 2200 km border with China (1342 miles) and a border with North Korea. Only several kilometers separate the Russian Far East between Sakhalin and Japan, or between Chukotka and Alaska.

On the following pages we provide basic information for each of the region's territories: Amur, Kamchatka, Khabarovsk, Magadan, Primorye, Yakutiia-Sakha, and Sakhalin.

AMUR OBLAST

Population:	1,062,500
Area:	363,700 sq. km.
Administrative Center:	Blagoveshchensk
Governor:	Vladimir Polevanov
Telephone:	(416-22) 2-47-69
Telex:	154111 PTB SU

Blagoveshchensk's (population: 214,000) major industries are construction, textiles and food-processing. It has established a flourishing border trade with the neighboring Chinese city of Heihe. Svobodnyi (81,000) on the Trans Siberian Railroad, with plentiful space for industrial development, is considered the most promising urban center in the oblast. Belogorsk (75,000) in the south is the agricultural center of Amur Oblast.

Economy and Industry

Amur Oblast is the granary of the Russian Far East, and dominates agriculture output in general. It accounts for almost 80% of Russia's soybean production. It contributes half of the Russian Far East's grain and flour output and a third of its dairy production. The oblast also has the largest hydropower generator in the Russian Far East — 1330 MW on the Zeya River dam, which enables it even to export power to Heihe — and a substantial, though stagnant, coal industry (5-6 million tons annually). Other key sectors include machine building (cranes, agricultural and mining), timber and construction materials.

Basic infrastructure

Two parallel railroads, the Trans Siberian and the Baikal-Amur lines, cross Amur Oblast, and are connected by the southernmost section of the uncompleted Amur-Yakutsk

Mainline. This makes the oblast second in railroad density in the Russian Far East. The region also takes advantage of an extensive river network, including 1250 km of waterway on the Amur River.

Geography and Climate

The climate in Amur Oblast is not too harsh. Permafrost in the north gives way to arable land in the plains of the Amur River valley (40% of the oblast). Average temperatures range from -28° (-18°F) in January to 19° (66°F) in July. The growing season is almost 170 days long.

Natural Resources

Large coal and iron-ore deposits make Amur Oblast the most suitable site for a long-planned integrated iron-and-steel complex in the Russian Far East. Other important resources include hydro power (a plant with a 2000 MW capacity has been under construction), nonferrous and rare metals, gold, quartz, kaolin, limestone, clay, tufa and almost 2 billion cubic meters of timber.

Prospects

The territory is a sleeper. It is relatively unknown to most foreign business and is well behind the coastal regions of the Russian Far East—in terms of foreign economic activity. From the point of view of foreign business interest, its relationship with China is most important. The planned construction of a bridge across the Amur into China will open the region to Northeast Asian business interests from the continent and should significantly boost development of the region.

Districts of Amur Oblast

Arkharinskii	20	Skovorodinskii	3
Belogorskii	10	Svobodnenskii	8
Blagoveshchenskii	11	Tambovskii	14
Bureiskii	19	Tyndinskii	1
Konstantinovskii	17	Uvanovskii	12
Magdagachinskii	4	Zavitinskii	16
Mazanovskii	6	Zeiskii	2
Mikhailovskii	18		
Oktiabrskii	15	**City-Districts**	
Romnenskii	13		
Selemdzhinskii	7	Blagoveshchensk	I
Seryshevskii	9	Raichikhinsk	II
Shimanovskii	5		

A Bit of History.

Beginning in the 1890's the reorganization of the Far East economy ... took place in the form of joint stock companies. Two large gold-mining conglomerates were formed before 1905: United Joint Gold Mining Company and the Amurskii Gold Mining Society.

In 1900, Amur oblast produced one fifth of the nation's gold. 200 mines were located here and the gold output reached 500 poods (1 pood = 36 pounds).

Capital was also concentrated in the food processing industry, especially
in flour milling and brewing. In 1900, Blagoveshchensk was the country's third largest producer of flour after Nizhnii Novgorod and Saratov, both cities located on the Volga.

Foreign capital played a role: for instance, local businessman Yuri Briner combined the rights to mine deposits of gold, coal and iron ore with German and French investors to build a successful company. The firm of Peppel and Ozimov was based on a similar combination of interests, this time in non-ferrous mining: Ozimov had the rights to mine, Peppel (a German) had the capital.

From **A History of the Far East of the USSR**
During Feudalism and Capitalism
A. Krushanov, Editor.

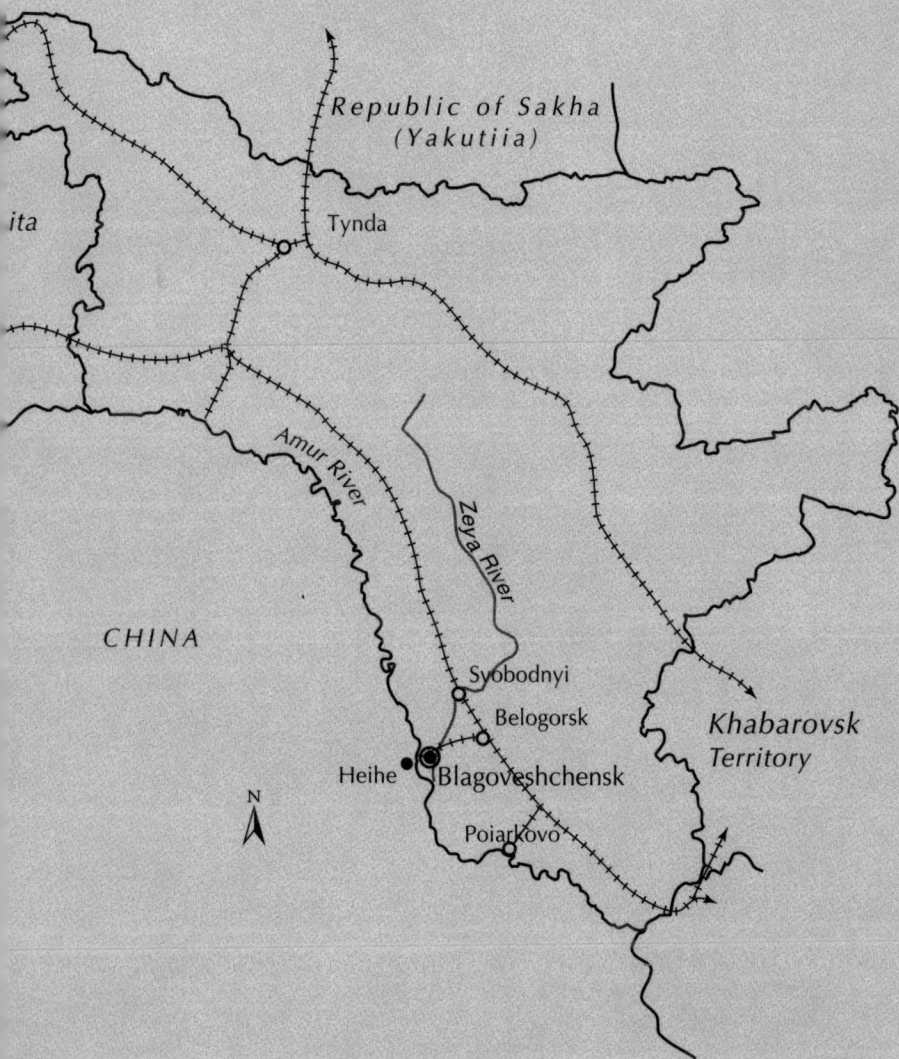

Republic of Sakha
(Yakutiia)

ita

Tynda

Amur River

Zeya River

CHINA

Svobodnyi

Belogorsk

Heihe   Blagoveshchensk

Khabarovsk
Territory

N

Poiarkovo

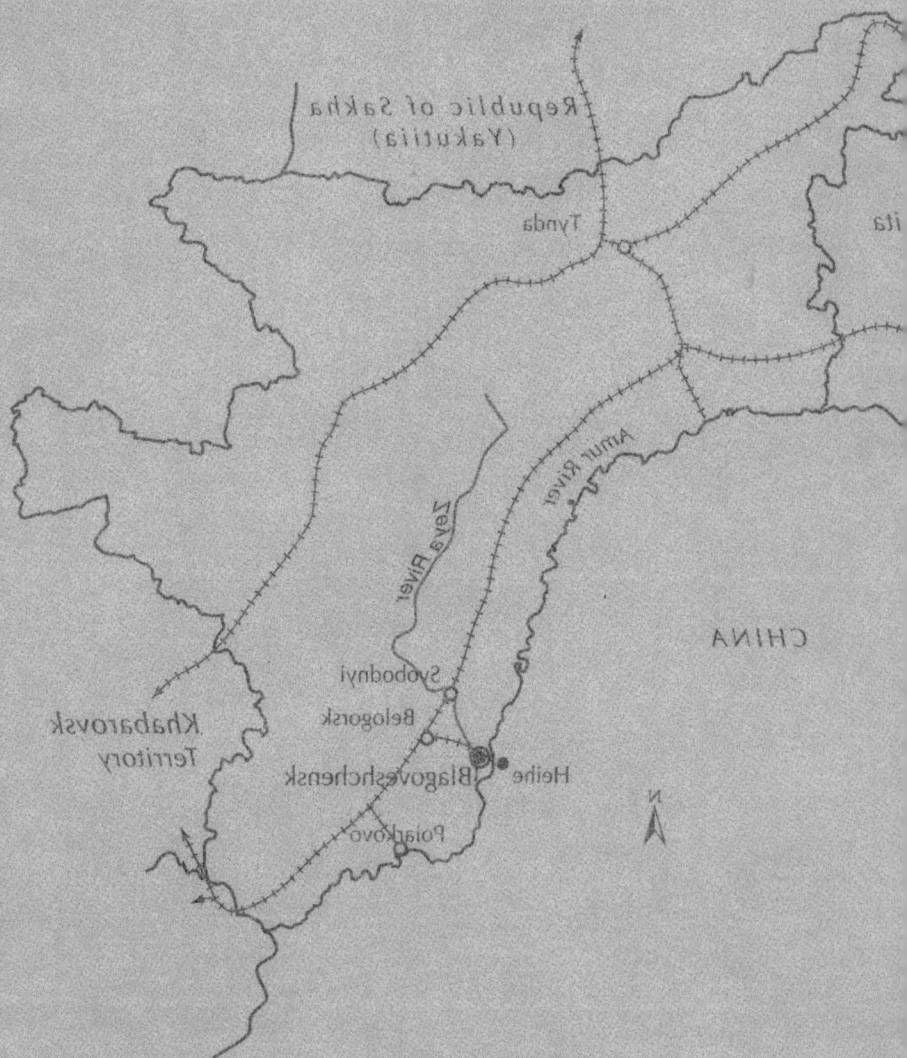

Republic of Sakha (Yakutia)

Tynda

Amur River

Zeya River

CHINA

Svobodnyi

Belogorsk

Heihe

Blagoveshchensk

Khabarovsk Territory

Poiarkovo

N

1

2

3

4

7

5

6

8

9

13

11

10

12

15

14   16   19

17   18

20

KAMCHATKA OBLAST

Population:	472,000
Area:	472,300 sq. km.
Administrative Center:	Petropavlovsk-Kamchatskii
Governor:	Vladimir A. Biriukov
Telephone:	(415-22) 2-20-96
Telex:	244124 INTUR SU

Petropavlovsk-Kamchatskii (population: 273,000), established in 1740 on the shores of Avacha Bay, is second to Primorye as a center for the Russian Far East fishing industry. It also is a base for nuclear submarines. Adjacent Elizovo (49,000) is the site of the oblast's international airport.

Economy and Industry

Kamchatka's dependency on a single industry is unusual — even for the undeveloped Russian Far East: 75% of the industrial output is produced by the fishing industry and another 9% — by the ship-repair sector that serves it. The oblast accounts for about 1/3 of the Russian Far East's total fish catch, and annually it produces about 1000 tons of salmon caviar (by far the most in Russia). However, fish processing facilities are less developed than in southern Primorskii Krai and almost 90% of the fishing fleet needs to be replaced. Other sectors of Kamchatka's economy are construction materials, forestry (0.4 million cubic meters of timber), reindeer husbandry and mink farming (100,000 pelts per year). One sector growing in importance is adventure tourism; visits to the Valley of the Geysers and to health resorts like Paratunka and Nachiki are becoming popular.

Basic Infrastructure

Because of the mountainous terrain, there are no railroads and very few major automobile roads on the peninsula. The airport at Elizovo provides helicopter service within the region, and has just recently received international status. The port of Korf, in the north of the peninsula on the Pacific Ocean, is open to international shipping and Petropavlovsk-Kamchatskii also can receive foreign vessels.

Geography and Climate

Surrounded by seas, Kamchatka has a mild climate, and cultivation of some crops is possible. 28 active volcanoes and the Russian Far East's highest level of seismic activity threaten Kamchatka's central and southern areas. Earthquake prevention currently performed by foreign firms costs up to $1000 per square foot of floorspace. Geysers and hot mineral springs are also present. Average temperatures range from -11° (+12°F) in February to 14° (57°F) in July. Average annual rainfall is 50 to 100 cm (20 to 40 in).

Natural resources

While rich in marine resources (especially crab and salmon), Kamchatka is completely dependent on imported fuel, although large deposits of coal have been found, and reserves of oil have been discovered off the western coast. Kamchatka boasts Russia's only geothermal power plant (11 MW). Among the minerals present are gold, silver, mercury, polymetals, sulfur and limestone.

Koryak Autonomous Okrug (38,000)

Administrative Center: Palana.

This area, which covers the northern half of the oblast, falls under the jurisdiction of Kamchatka Oblast. It is mainly populated by Russians (62%); the native Koryaks make up 16% of the population. Large gold deposits were recently discovered here.

Prospects

Kamchatka is astir with development aspirations. Foreigners are waiting to cooperate. Administration and local entrepreneurs (sometimes you cannot tell the difference) are interested in the gains from international market trade. We can expect to see much more activity happening here soon.

Kamchatka Peninsula

A. Districts of Kamchatka Oblast		B. Districts of Koriak Autonomous	
Aleutskii	9	Okrug	
Bystrinskii	6	Karaginskii	3
Elizovskii	10	Oliutorskii	2
Milkovskii	8	Penzhinskii	1
Sobolevskii	7	Tigilskii	4
Ust-Bolsheretskii	11		
Ust-Kamchatskii	5		

A Bit of History.

In 1865-67 George Kennan led an expedition for the Western Union Telegraph Company to Kamchatka and Chukotka. The Company had planned to build an overland telegraph line to Europe via Alaska, the Bering Straits and Siberia. The project was aborted when news came that the Atlantic cable had been successfully laid. Kennan's travels were recorded in his book, Tent Life in Siberia (Salt Lake City: Gibbs M. Smith, Inc., 1986). Some of the telegraph poles are still standing and can be seen from helicopter in Northern Magadan.

1865: For nearly an hour Dodd and I sat quietly on the beach... With what different impressions had I come to look at life since I first saw the precipitous coast of Kamchatka. Then it was an unknown, mysterious land of glaciers and snowy mountains, filled with possibilities of adventure, but lonely and forbidding it in its uninhabited wilderness. Now it was no longer lonely or desolate. Every mountain peak was associated with some hospitable village nestled at its feet; every stream was connected with the great world of human interests by some pleasant recollection of camp life. The possibilities of adventure were still there, but the imaginary loneliness and desolation had vanished with one week's experience.

From **Tent Life in Siberia**
George Kennan

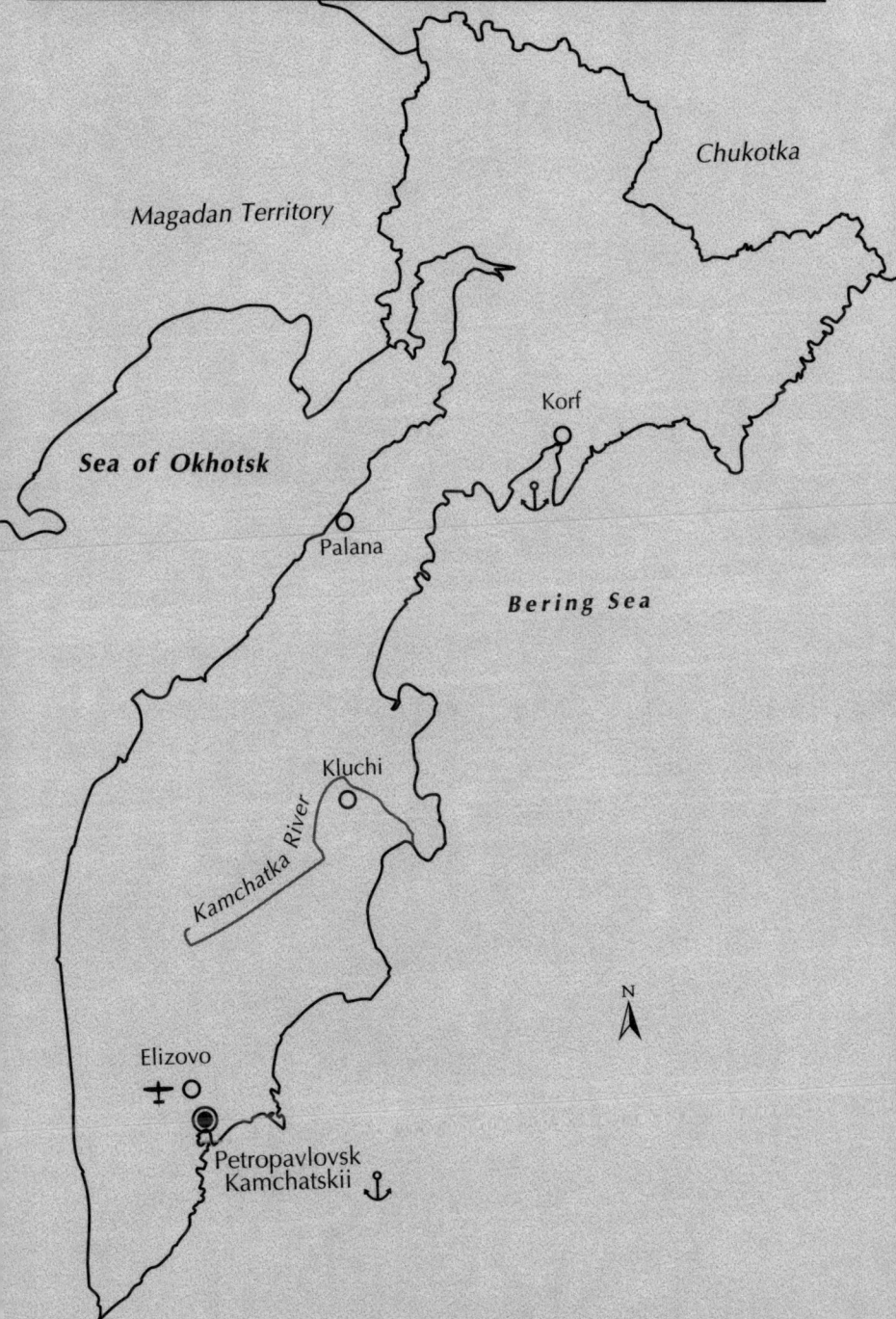

Chukotka

Magadan Territory

Sea of Okhotsk

Korf

Palana

Bering Sea

Kluchi

Kamchatka River

N

Elizovo

Petropavlovsk
Kamchatskii

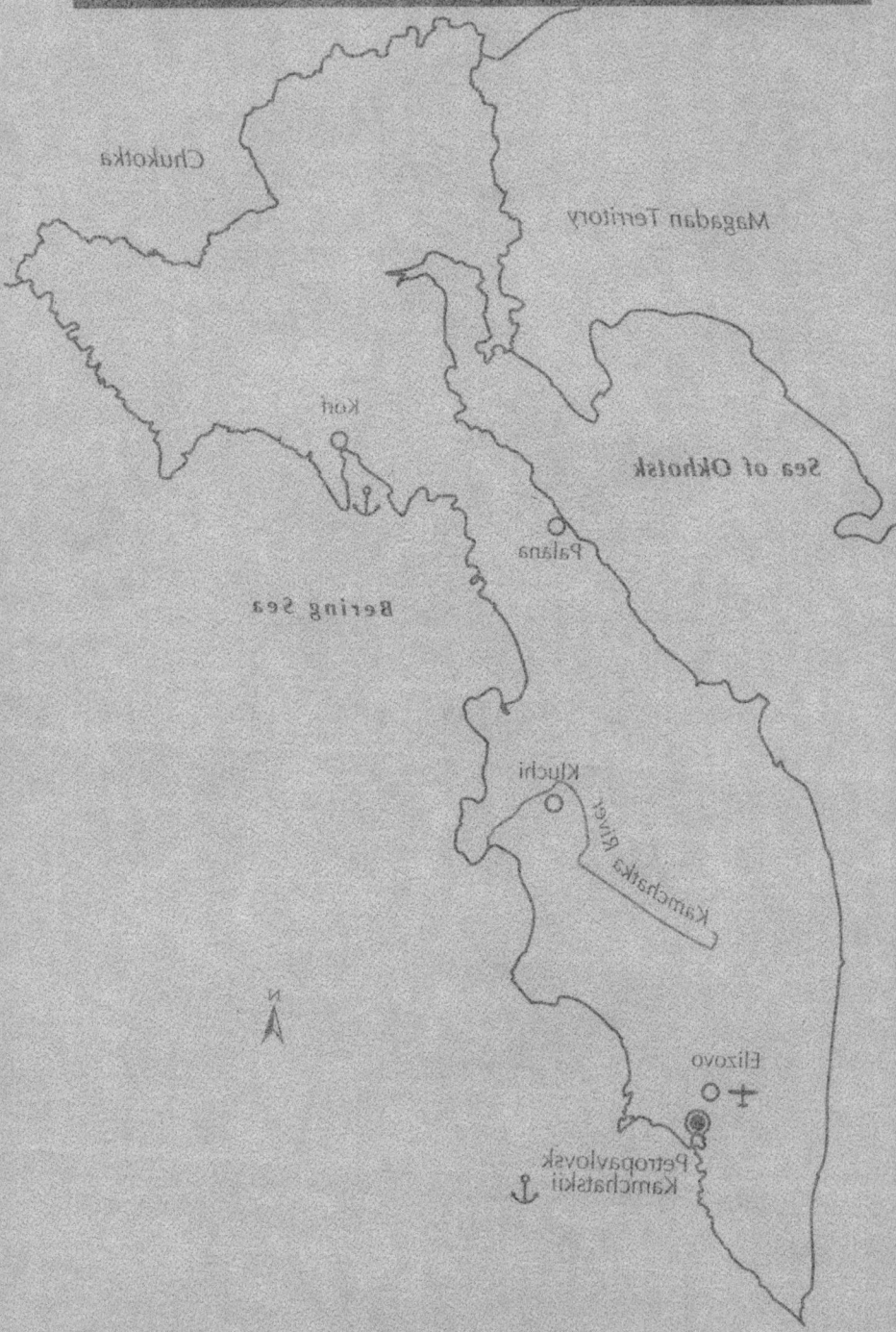

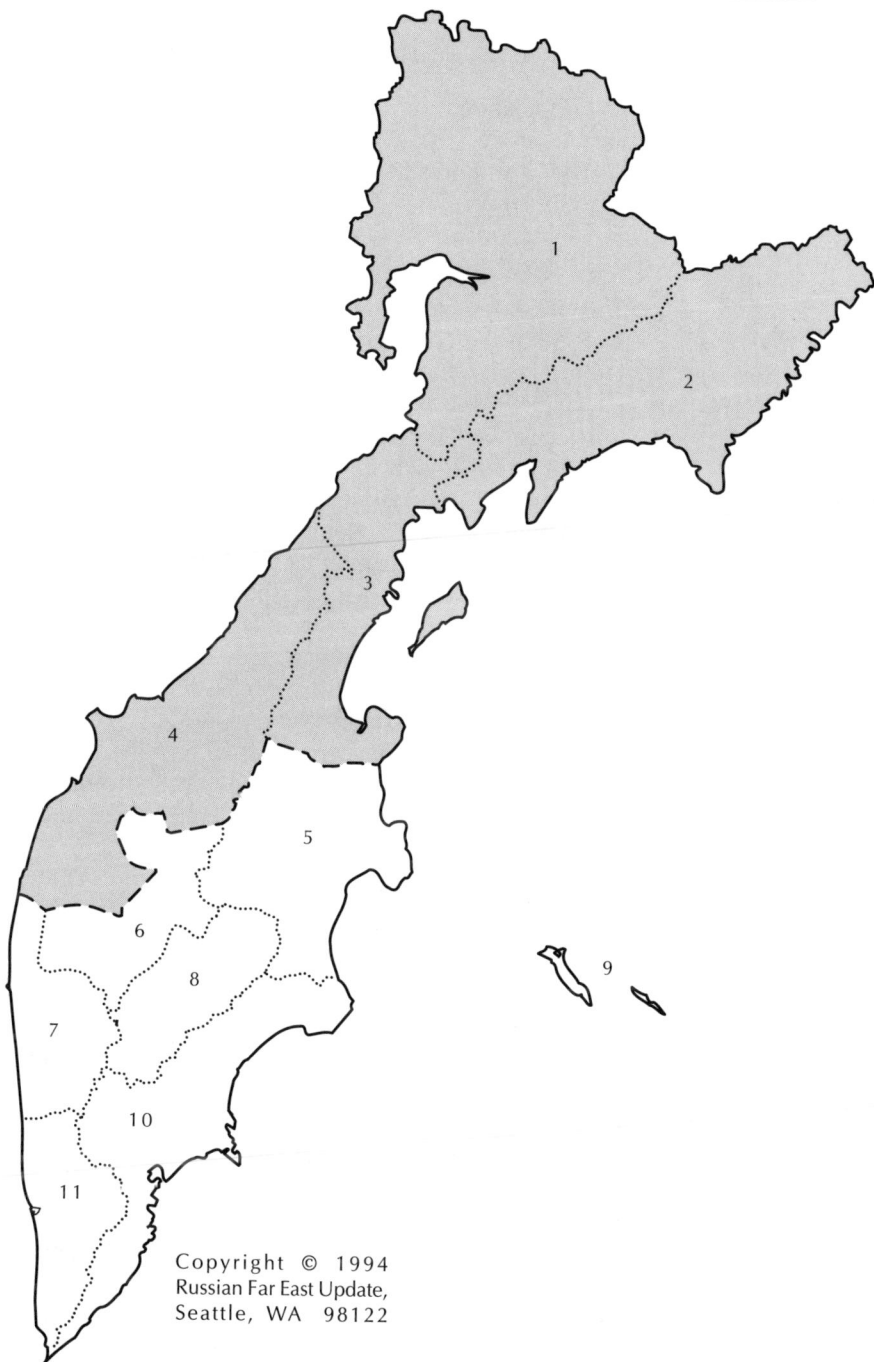

KHABAROVSK KRAI

Population:	1,840,400
Area:	824,000 sq. km.
Administrative Center:	Khabarovsk
Governor:	Victor Ishaev
Telephone:	(421-2) 33-50-40
Telex:	141131 ASTRA SU

The city of Khabarovsk (population: 615,000) was founded in 1858 at the confluence of the Amur and Ussuri Rivers. Until recently this major transportation hub was the only city in the Russian Far East open to foreigners. The city is the Russian Far East's largest center for civilian machine building; its 100 plants (much in need of modernization) turn out lathes, turbines, diesel engines, ships, cable, fish-processing equipment and more. Komsomolsk-on-Amure (319,000) heads an industrial region that generates 40% of the krai's output. Its 40 major factories produce iron & steel, oil products, ocean-going vessels, machinery, lumber, apparel and lots of military hardware. Nearby Amursk (60,000), also an important defense-industry center, has the Russian Far East's largest pulp and paperboard plant. Sovetskaya Gavan (35,000), with two ship-repair yards, and the krai's main seaport of Vanino (18,000) form the third industrial center. Nikolaevsk-on-Amure (36,500), the krai's oldest city, long ago lost its importance as a port.

Economy and Industry

Khabarovsk Krai is the only region in the Russian Far East where civilian machine building dominates industry (30%). Its huge specialized plants have produced more equipment than almost all of the rest of the Russian Far East put together. What's missing is product for the local market. Therefore, reorientation of the krai's heavy industry is of increasing importance. The krai's timber industry leads the Russian Far East in logging and lumber production. The krai has the biggest energy deficit in the Russian Far East. It has the Russian Far East's only iron & steel plant (1.0-1.1 million tons per year) and both Russian Far East oil refineries.

Basic Infrastructure

Two major railways cross the territory — the Trans-Siberian Railroad and the Baikal-Amur Mainline (BAM). An international airport at Khabarovsk, handling 4 million passengers per year, is the eastern gateway to Russia. The Amur River Steamship company, which operates on the Amur River, carries 20% of Russia's trade with Japan. The port of Vanino (open to international shipping), the terminus of the BAM and main supply point for Sakhalin (through a ferry), is now planning for expansion.

Geography and Climate

The mountainous krai is covered by forests (taiga) consisting mainly of larch, spruce and fir. The Amur River is a main channel for transport. Winters are dry, with little snow, and summers are humid. Average temperatures in the southern krai range from -22° (-8°F) in January to 21° (70°F) in July.

Natural Resources

Khabarovskii Krai has 5.3 billion cubic meters of high-quality timber (85% coniferous), coal, gold, tin, manganese, tungsten and molybdenum.

Jewish Autonomous Oblast   (219,400)

Administrative Center: Birobidzhan (pop. 87,000)
Governor: Nikolai Volkov
Phone: (42162) 60242

This compact region in SW Khabarovsk Krai is now politically independent from the krai. Only 4% of the population is Jewish. The JAO's economy is mostly agricultural, but Birobidzhan is the Russian Far East's largest center of light industry. Border trade with China is increasing.

Prospects

Local policy-makers sometimes seem stymied by the sheer weight of the region's problems, but the administration espouses a "friendly" investment environment. Two important potential developments here: (1) the possible opening of the region's defense industries to international investment in the cities of Komsomolsk-on-Amure and nearby Amursk; (2) the prospective development of the region's transportation infrastructure, especially railroad/seaport complex at Vanino.

Districts of Khabarovsk Krai

Aiano-Maiskii	2	Tugoro-Chumikanskii	3
Amurskii	10	Ulchskii	6
Bikinskii	17	Vaninskii	12
im. Lazo	15	Verkhnebureinskii	7
im. Poliny Osipenko	5	Viazemskii	16
Khabarovskii	13		
Komsomolskii	9		

Jewish Autonomous Oblast

Nanaiskii	11	Birobidzhanskii	D
Nikolaevskii	4	Leninskii	C
Okhotskii	1	Obluchenskii	A
Solnechnyi	8	Oktiabrskii	B
Sovetsko-Gavanskii	14	Smidovichskii	E

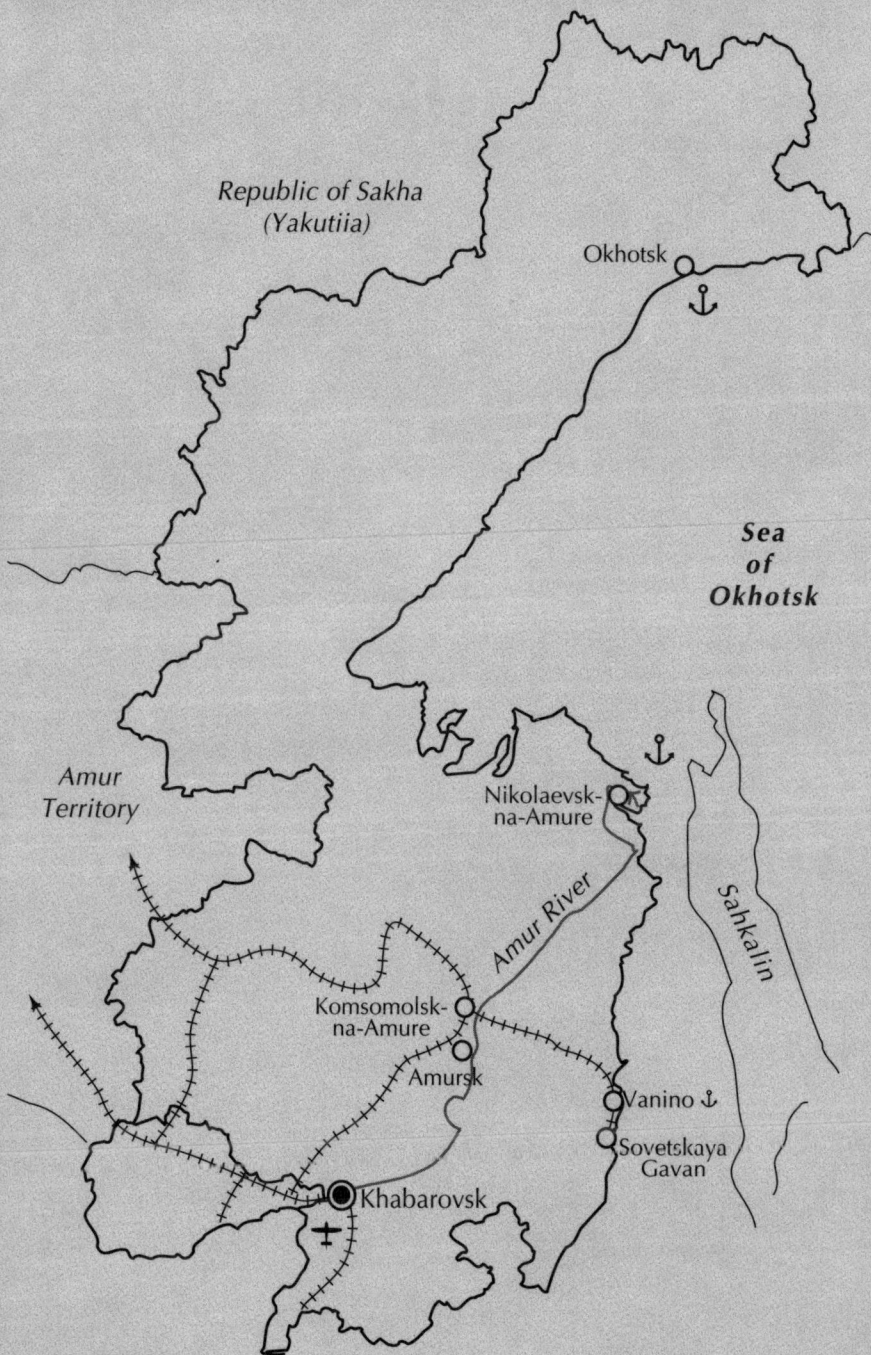

Republic of Sakha
(Yakutiia)

Okhotsk

Sea
of
Okhotsk

Amur
Territory

Nikolaevsk-
na-Amure

Amur River

Sahkalin

Komsomolsk-
na-Amure

Amursk

Vanino

Sovetskaya
Gavan

Khabarovsk

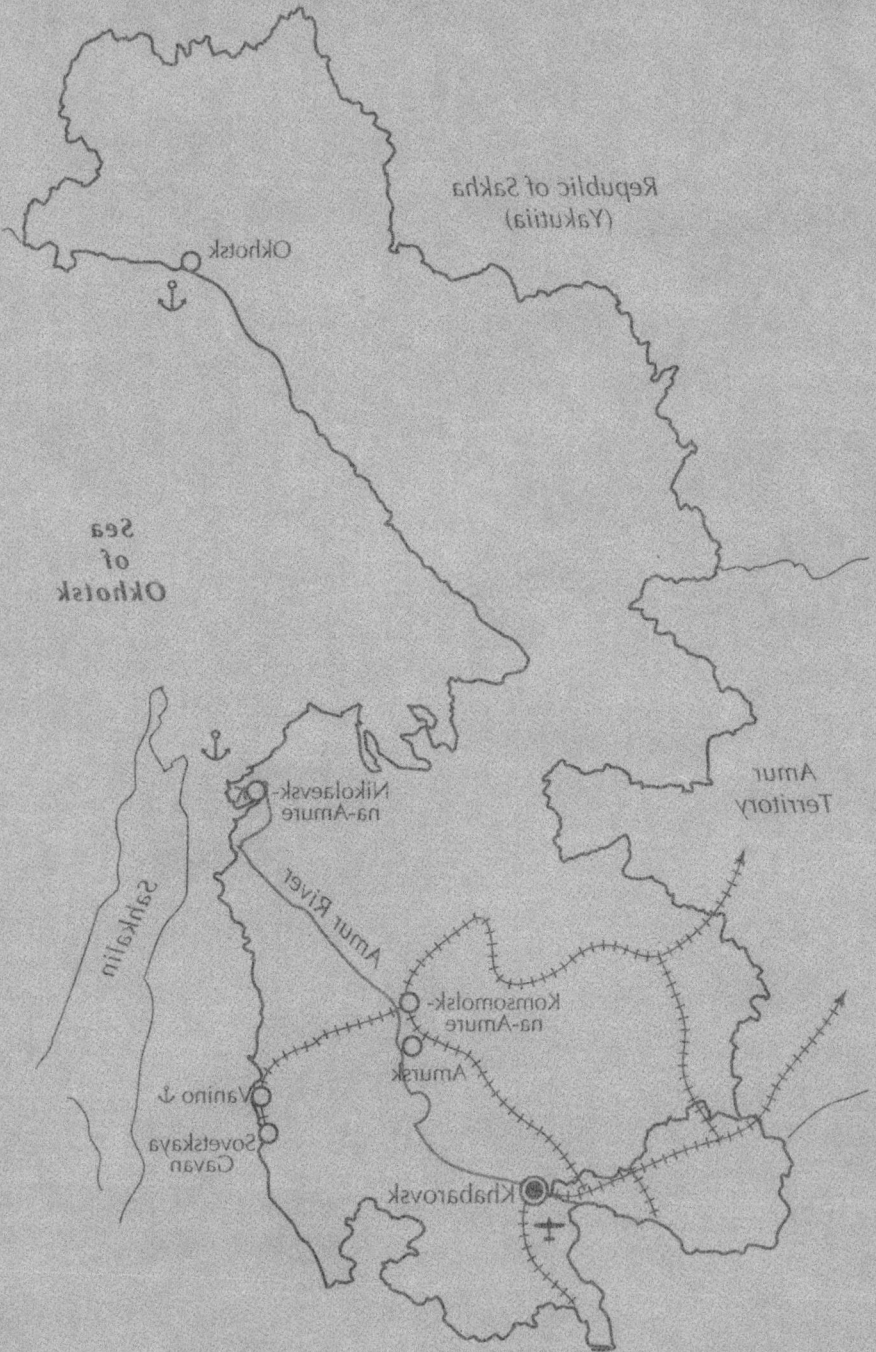

Republic of Sakha
(Yakutia)

Okhotsk

Sea
of
Okhotsk

Amur
Territory

Nikolaevsk-
na-Amure

Sakhalin

Amur River

Komsomolsk-
na-Amure

Amursk

Vanino

Sovetskaya
Gavan

Khabarovsk

1

2

3

4

5

6

7

8

9

10

11

12

13

A

B C D E

13
○ Khabarovsk

14

15

16

17

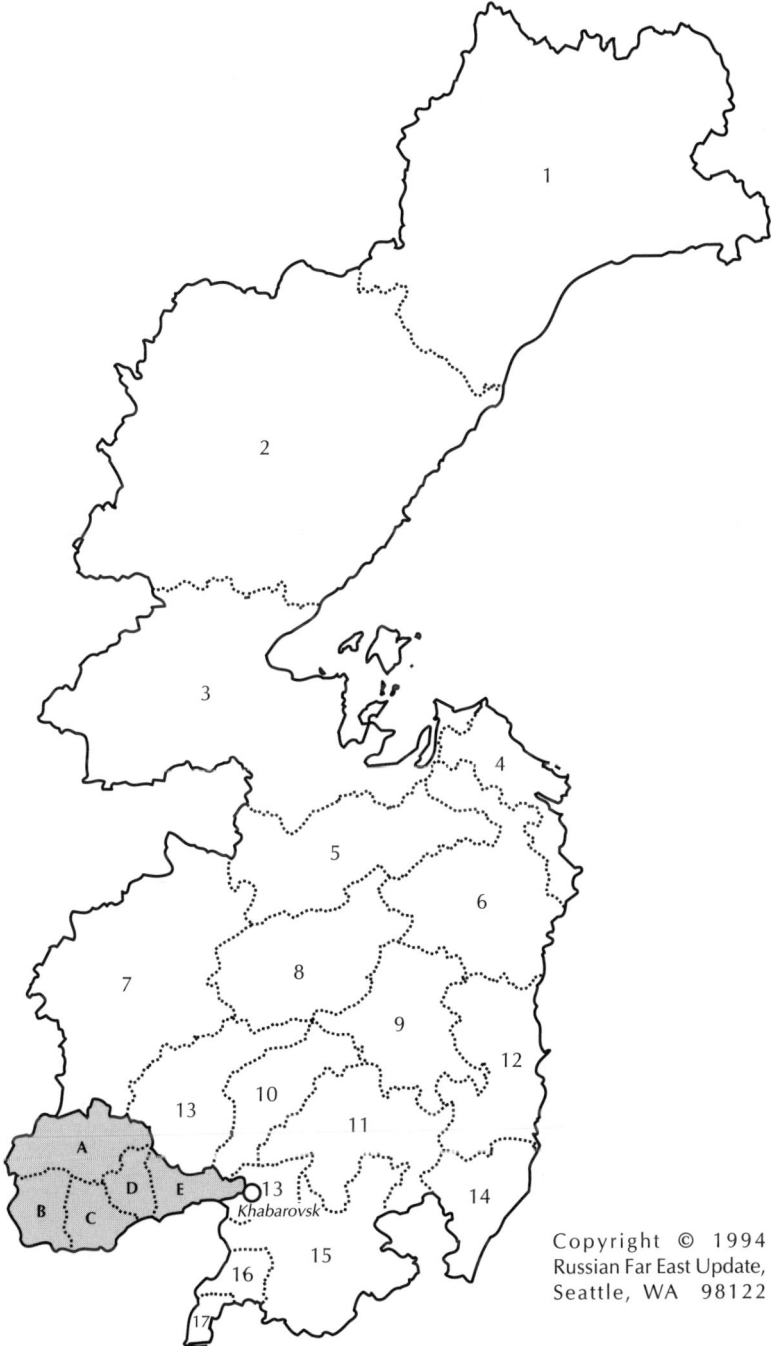

MAGADAN OBLAST

Population:	550,800
Area:	1,199,100 sq. km.
Administrative Center:	Magadan
Governor:	Victor Mikhailov
Telephone:	(413-00) 2-31-34
Telex:	145 119 SOVET SU

The city of Magadan (population: 152,000) was founded in 1933 as a transit point for political prisoners bound for the Kolyma gold fields. The city is now the biggest port in the Russian Northeast. Magadan's port, Nagayevo, has a large fishing fleet, and remains open year-round with the help of icebreakers. Susuman (16,800) is the center of the Kolyma mining basin.

Economy and Industry

The economy here is narrowly based and the most stagnant in all the Russian Far East. Mining accounts for almost 60% of industrial output. The oblast has been among Russia's leading producers of gold, silver, and tin and tungsten, but production is shifting to Chukotka from the depleted Kolyma valley. Magadan and Chukotka produced 43 tons of gold in 1992, 33% of Russia's total.

Second in importance is energy production. The Russian Far East's only nuclear power station is located at Bilibino (installed capacity 48MW). Three million tons of coal are mined yearly, part of which is hauled by truck to Sakha. Other sectors are the fishing industry, and machine building for the mines.

Agriculture is centered on reindeer husbandry and mink farms (mink farms yield around 100,000 pelts annually). Foreign tourism is gaining importance, with Alaska Airlines and Aeroflot now flying to Magadan from San Francisco, Seattle and Anchorage.

Basic Infrastructure

There are no railroads, but the all-weather Kolymskaia highway links the resource-rich Kolyma basin with the port at Magadan. Airports at Magadan, Anadyr and Provideniya in Chukotka are open to international flights.

Geography and Climate

Magadansakaya Oblast and Chukotka are the closest Russian territories to Alaska. Permafrost and tundra cover most of the region, ruling out any open-earth cultivation; the growing season is only 100 days long, so almost all food must be supplied from without. Average temperatures on the coast of the Sea of Okhotsk range from -22° (-8°F) in January to 12° (54°F) in July, and in the interior, from -38° (-36°F) to 16° (60°F).

Natural Resources

Gold, coal, tin, tungsten (second in reserves in the Russian Far East), mercury, coal, reindeer and fish.

Prospects

The opening of relations between Alaska and Magadan was signficant for Magadan. However, the goodwill generated over the last several years between the two regions cannot by itself bring about economic development. The region's mineral resources are the issue. Local administrators have been fairly bold in their attempts to attract foreign investment.

Chukotska Autonomous Oblast   (124,000)

Administrative Center: Anadyr (17,130)
Governor: Alexander Nazarov
Phone: (41361) 42126

Chukotskaya Autonomous Okrug formerly was the NE half of Magadan Oblast. In 1992 the Russian parliament recognized Chukotka's separation from Magadan. Chukotka produces substantial quantities of gold. Pevek (13,020) is Chukotka's main Arctic port, servicing a rich tin-mining region.

Districts of Magadan Oblast

Khasynskii	5
Olskii	6
Omsukchanskii	7
Severo-Evenskii	8
Srednekanskii	3
Susumanskii	1
Tenkinskii	4
Yarodninskii	6

City-Districts
| Magadan | I |

Districts of Chukotka Autonomous Oblast

Anadyrskii	15
Beringovskii	16
Bilibinskii	9
Chaunskii	10
Chukotskii	13
Providenskii	14
Shmidtovskii	11
Yiultinskii	12

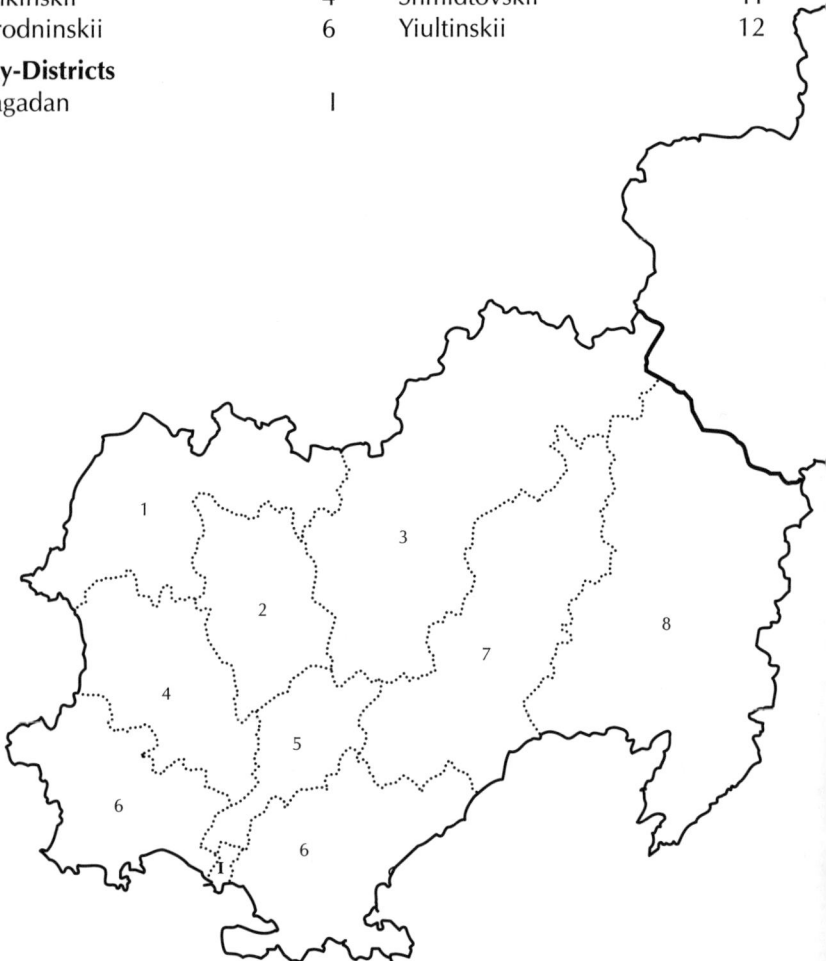

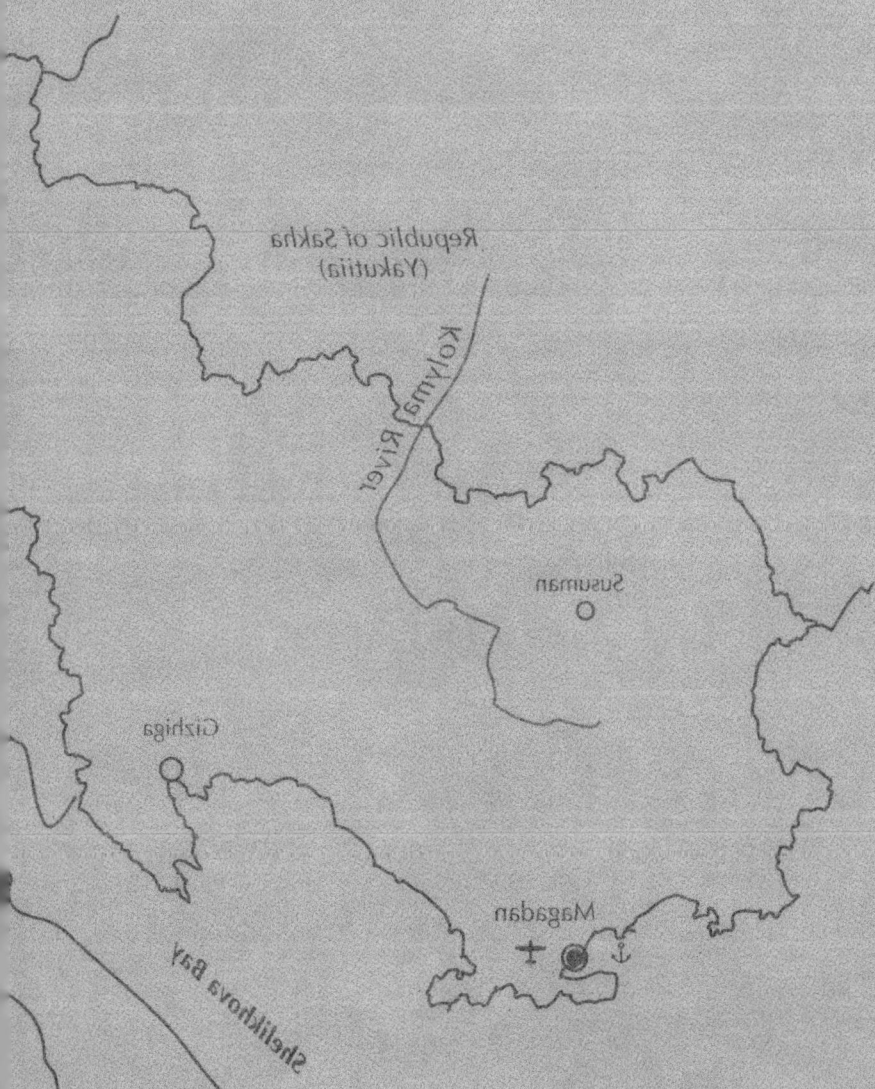

Republic of Sakha
(Yakutia)

Kolyma River

Susuman

Gizhiga

Magadan

Shelikhova Bay

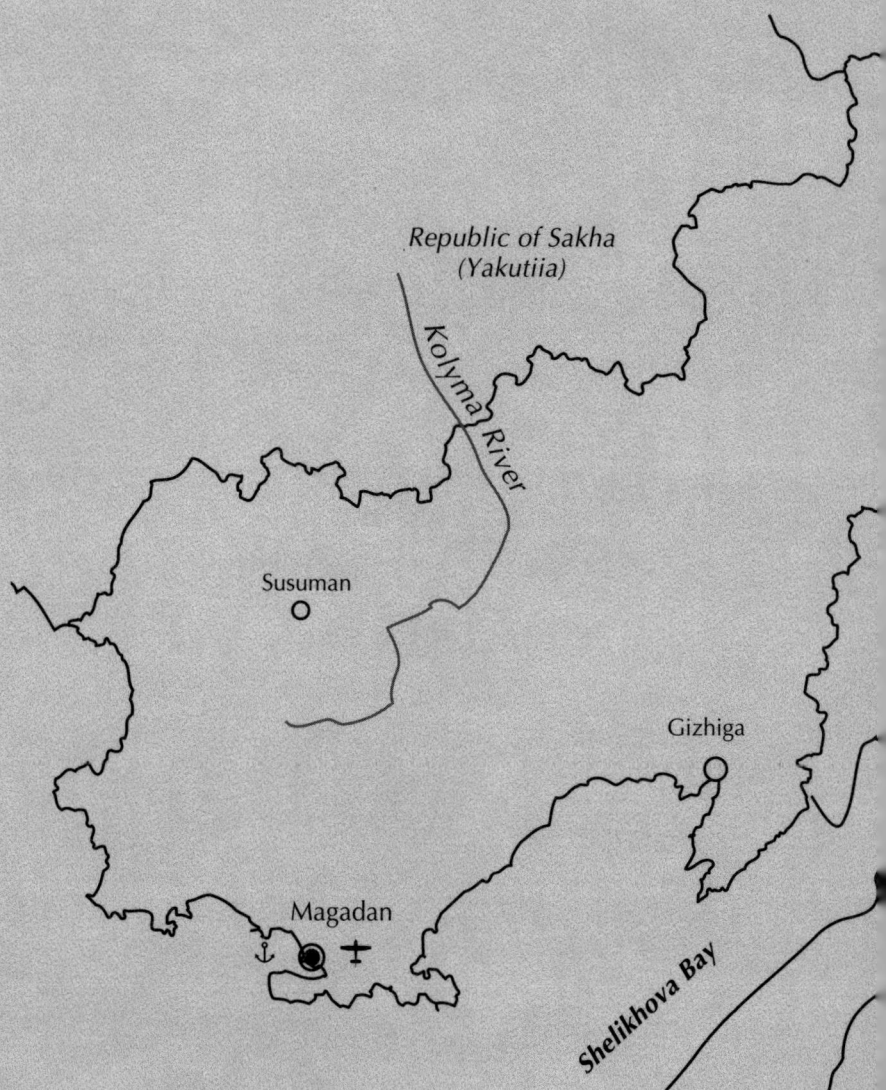

*Republic of Sakha
(Yakutiia)*

Kolyma River

Susuman
○

Gizhiga
○

Magadan
●

Shelikhova Bay

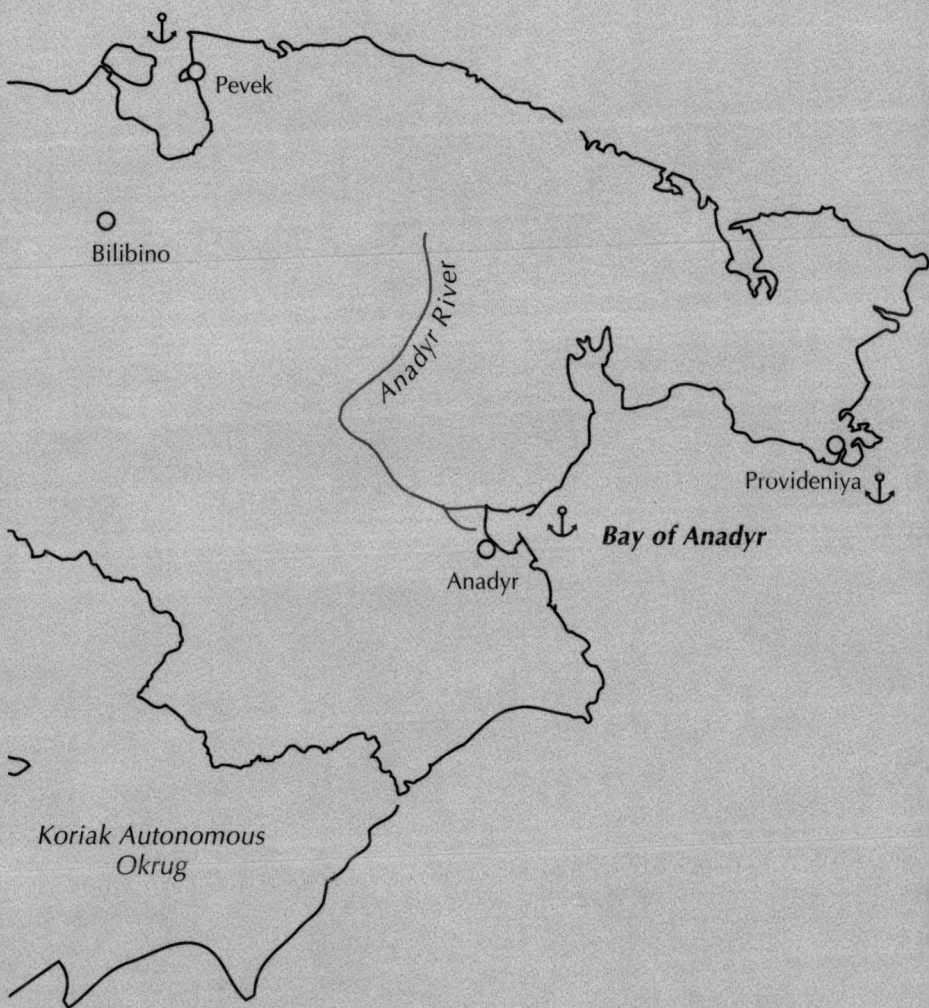

MAGADAN

Pevek

Bilibino

Anadyr River

Provideniya

Bay of Anadyr

Anadyr

Koriak Autonomous
Okrug

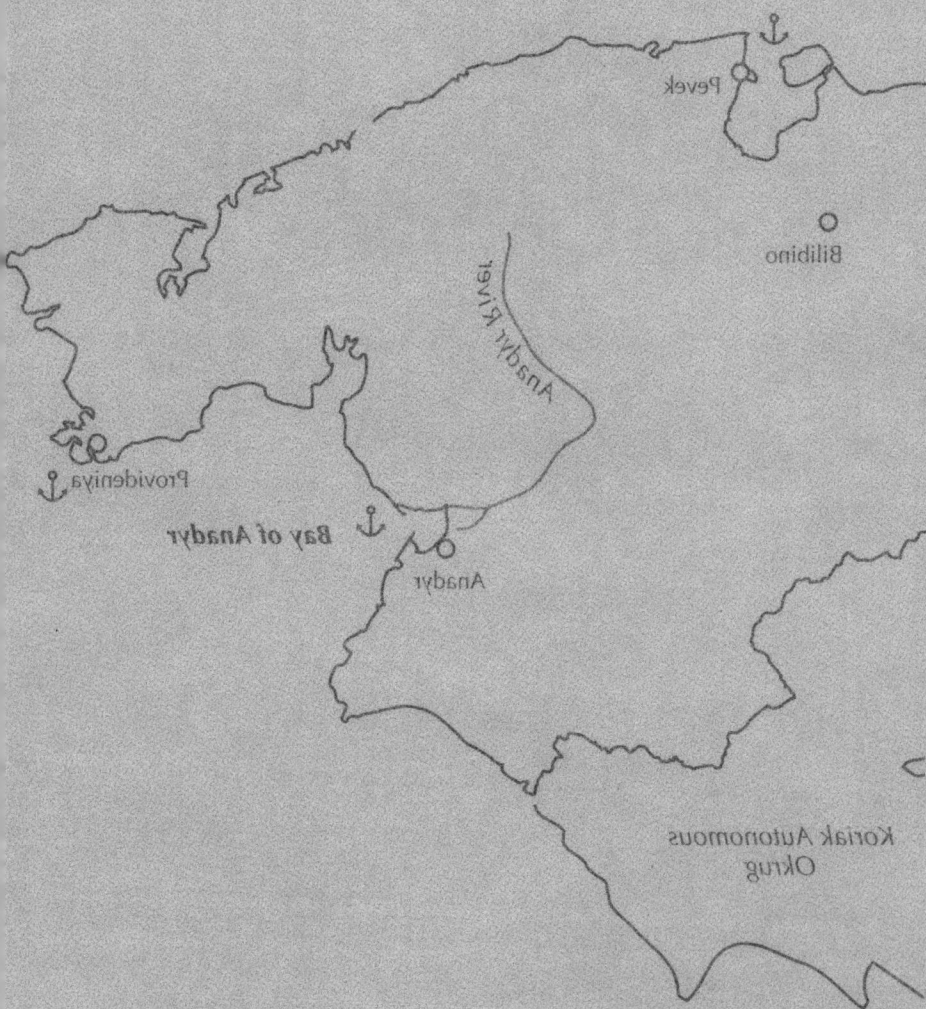

Okrug

PRIMORYE

Population:	2,301,700
Area:	165,900 sq. km.
Other names:	Maritime Region, Primorskii Krai
Administrative Center:	Vladivostok
Governor:	Evgenii Nazdratenko
Telephone:	(423-2) 22-38-00
Telex:	213 216 GROM SU

Vladivostok (population: 648,000) was founded in 1860 and is home of the Russian Pacific Fleet and the Far Eastern Shipping Company (FESCO). Fish-processing, ship repair and the defense industry dominate the city's economy. Nakhodka (166,000) and Vostochnyi (15,000) have Russia's biggest fish canneries. Ussuriisk (161,000) is a center of food processing. Arsenev (72,000) produces military aircraft and navigational equipment. Two plants in Spassk-Dalnii (61,000) produce half of the Russian Far East's cement output. The Kavalerovo-Dalnegorsk mining center turns out tin, lead, zinc and boron.

Economy and Industry

Primorye's economy, the most balanced in the Russian Far East, is also the largest in absolute terms. Food production is the most important sector, represented mainly by fish processing. Annual catch fluctuates around 1.5-2 million tons, or one half of the Russian Far East total. Second is machine building, where half the output is geared toward the fishing industry and shipyards. Defense is another important sector, producing naval vessels and military aircraft. The construction-materials industry here provides for the whole Russian Far East.

The timber industry, though in deep crisis, is still second only to Khabarovskii Krai with an annual yield of about 3 million cubic meters of timber. Primorskii Krai mines 12-13 million tons of coal, slightly more than Sakha and generates more electricity (11 billion kW) than any other Russian Far East province, but power shortages are common. Agriculture makes the krai the Russian Far East's leading producer of rice, milk, eggs and vegetables. The krai's proximity to Pacific Rim markets give it an edge over other Russian Far East provinces in developing foreign trade: it is the Russian Far East leader in terms of total foreign trade.

Basic Infrastructure

Primorye's compact territory is well endowed with infrastructure. Its railway density is twice the Russian average. Railroads connect it with China and North Korea. Vladivostok, the eastern terminus of the Trans-Siberian Railway, was surpassed as a port by the nearby Nakhodka-Vostochnyi complex of container, coal and timber terminals. Primorye-based shipping companies provide 80% of marine shipping services in the Russian Far East and its ports account for 50% of all Russian facilities. All the krai's ports of significance are now open to international shipping. All are in need of modernization. Inefficiency and bottlenecks remain one of the most serious deterrents to growth.

Geography and Climate

Primorye, bordered by the Sea of Japan, and the countries of China and North Korea, lies just 400 miles from Japan. In the south the coast is jagged with many bays and inlets. Most of the territory is mountainous, and almost 80% is forested. Winters are short but cold; summers are cloudy, rainy, with frequent cyclones. The growing season in the south is 200 days long. Average temperatures range from -20° (-40° F) in January to 20° (68°F) in July.

Natural Resources

Primorye is endowed with more than 2 billion tons of coal, 1.7 billion cubic meters of timber (including 0.5 billion cubic meters of valuable cedar), large tin, fluoride and bromide deposits, newly expanded reserves of lead and zinc, two tungsten deposits and abundant marine resources.

Prospects

With the opening of Vladivostok in 1992, the region now has a very important stimulus for the creation of an effective economic development policy. The ever present question: Will the region be able to create such a policy and get Moscow's support?

Districts of Primorskii Krai

Anuchinskii	18	Olginskii	20
Chernigovskii	11	Partizanskii	24
Chuguevskii	13	Pogranichnyi	9
Dalnegorskii	15	Pozharskii	1
Dalnerechenskii	2	Shkotovskii	23
Kavalerovskii	14	Spasskii	8
Khankaiskii	7	Terneiskii	6
Khasanskii	22	Ussuriiskii	19
Khorolskii	10	Yakovlevskii	12
Kirovskii	5		

City-Districts

Krasnoarmeiskii	3
Lazovskii	25
Lesozavodskii	4
Mikhailovskii	17
Nadezhdinskii	21
Oktiabrskii	16

Arsenev	II
Artem	III
Dalnerechensk	I
Nakhodka	VI
Partizansk	V
Vladivostok	IV

A Bit of History

1888: Despite several petitions from the City of Vladivostok since 1880 for approval of its development plans, not even a commission has been named which would be required for approval and implementation.

Since 1883 several city blocks and much good land have been set aside by local authorities; yet minor officials from several different government departments have been using land for their own particular purposes — without any reference to a general plan.

The city doesn't have enough space for the new commercial port and docks that it needs. Its best hope is to get the property on which the old port is now located. But this requires military approval. Meanwhile, property around the old port is being used by several commercial enterprises of the Shipping Fleet and enterprises owned by the well-known entrepreneur Shevelev.

from ***A Short Historical Sketch of the City of Vladivostok***,
Matveyev 1990

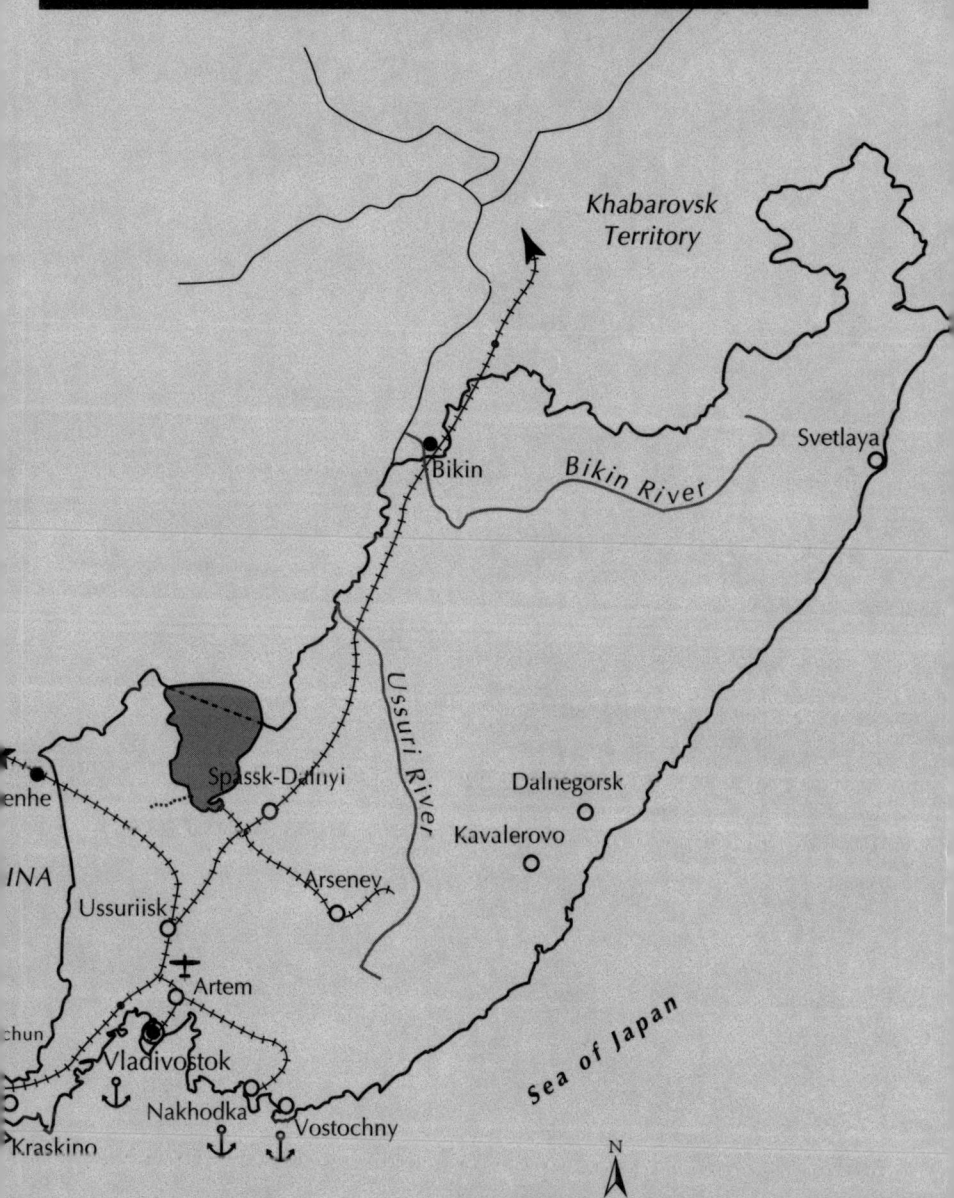

Khabarovsk
Territory

Svetlaya

Bikin

Bikin River

Ussuri River

Dalnegorsk

Spassk-Dalnyi

Kavalerovo

enhe

Arseney

INA

Ussuriisk

Artem

chun

Vladivostok

Nakhodka

Vostochny

Kraskino

Sea of Japan

N

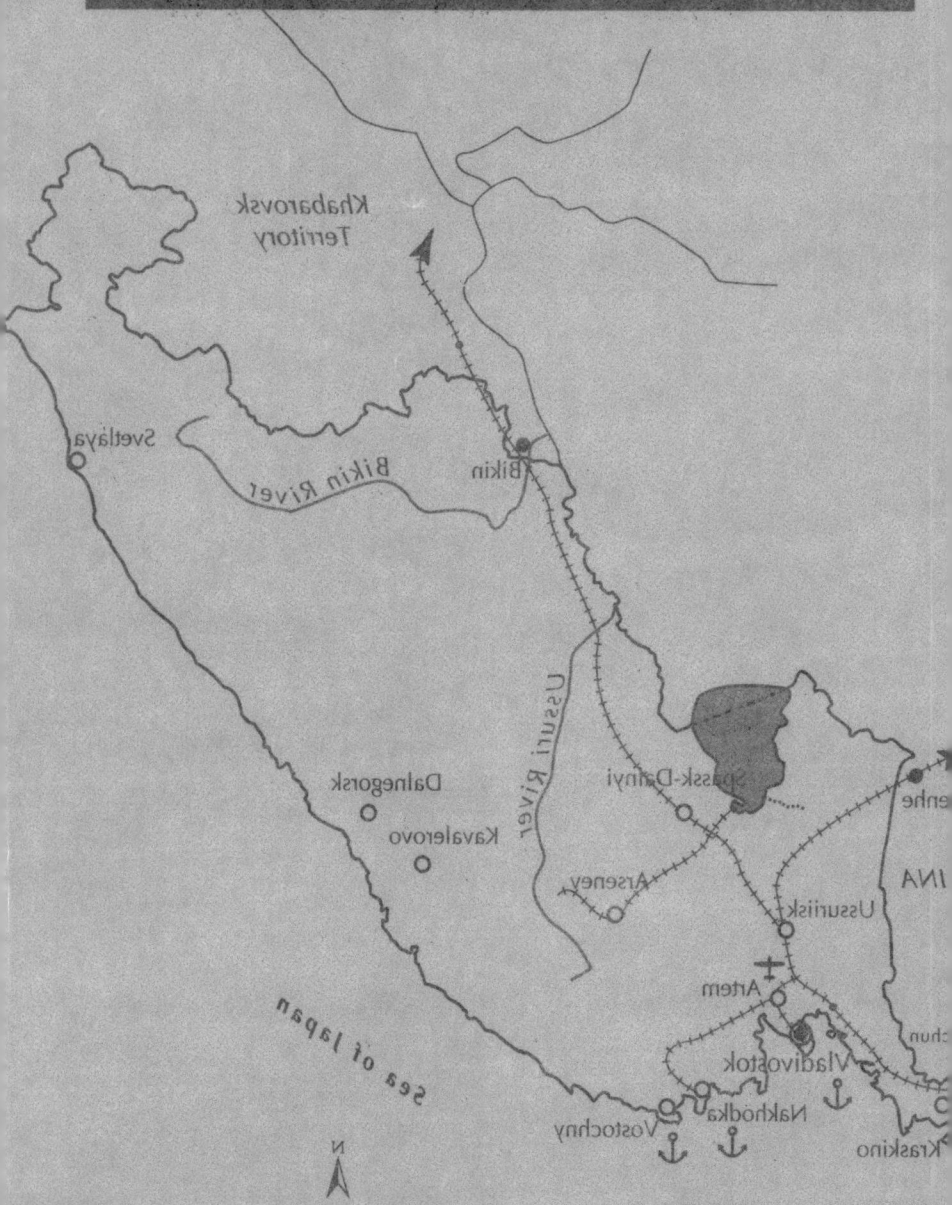

Khabarovsk
Territory

Svetlaya

Bikin River

Bikin

Ussuri River

Dalnegorsk

Kavalerovo

Spassk-Dalnyi

Arseney

Ussuriisk

Artem

Vladivostok

Nakhodka

Vostochny

Kraskino

Sea of Japan

N

INA

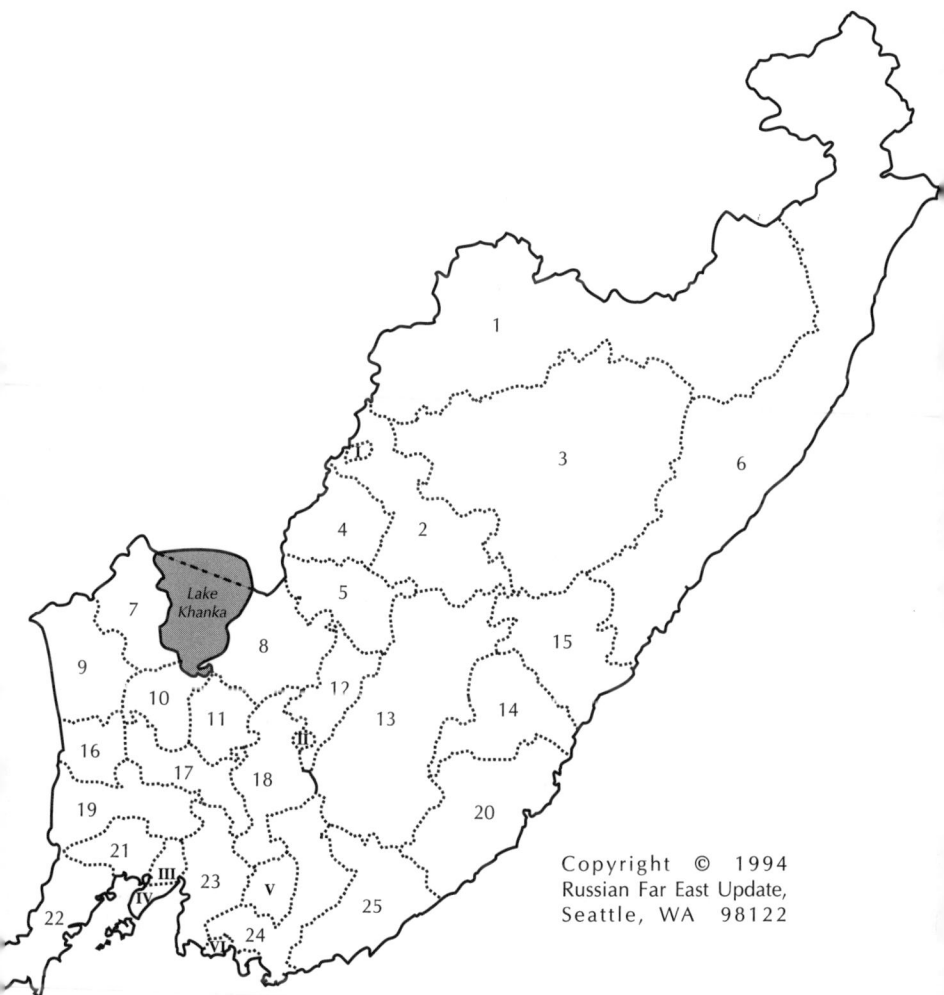

1

I

3

6

4

2

5

Lake
Khanka

7

8

15

9

10

12

13

14

16

11

II

17

18

20

19

21

III

23

V

22

IV

24

25

VI

REPUBLIC OF YAKUTIIA-SAKHA

Population:	1,073,800
Area:	3,103,200 sq. km.
Former name:	Yakutiia
Capital:	Yakutsk
President:	Mikhail Nikolaev
Address:	Kirov Street, 10

The city of Yakutsk (population:198,000), founded as a fort on the Lena River in 1632, has served as a supply base for northeastern Russia for centuries. It is probably the only large city completely built on permafrost. Major industries include construction-materials production, meat, timber and fur. Neryungri (76,000) in the south, with an open-pit coal mine (capacity: 13 million tons, some of which is exported to Japan) feeds a large thermal power plant. Mirnyi (40,000) in the west is the center of one of the world's richest diamond-mining areas, and Aldan (27,400) in the south services a large gold-mining region. Lensk (31,200) in SW Sakha is an important river port.

Economy and Industry

Before the current industrial slowdown, Sakha's industry was one of the fastest growing in the Russian Far East. Sakha is Russia's principal producer of diamonds, gold and tin. As the most accessible gold and diamond deposits have been exhausted, mining costs are now increasing. Yakutiia mines a quarter of Russia's gold. Tin mining is important and has good prospects.

Next in importance are energy fuels. Sakha is the region's second leading producer of coal (about 12 million tons annually, of which about 4 million is exported). In natural gas production (1.5 billion cubic meters), it is second to Sakhalin. Other important economic sectors are construction materials, logging (annual deliveries of 2.5 million cubic meters) and food processing. Sakha also provides approximately one fifth of Russia's fur output.

Basic Infrastructure

Sakha, five times the size of Texas, has rudimentary infrastructure. Rivers are navigable five months of the year, and serve as roadways when frozen. Summer shipping on the 4400 km-long Lena River and on other rivers is still the chief method of transport. Approximately one-third of the Amur-Yakutsk Mainline railway is completed (work began in 1985), but lack of funds is delaying progress.

Geography and Climate

All the republic is covered in permafrost; 44% of its land area is within the Arctic Circle. Cut off from the sea to the east by steep mountains, Sakha has the most extreme temperature conditions in the Northern Hemisphere. Winters are cold, dry and windless. Summers are short, with intermittent heat waves. Average temperatures range from -40° (-40°F) in January to 13° (55°F) in July. The growing season ranges from 60 to 130 days. Verkhoyansk has recorded temperatures ranging from -70° (-94°F) to 35° (95°F), and Yakutsk, the capital, from -64° (-83°F) to 38° (100°F).

Natural Resources

Sakha until recently was Russia's only source of diamonds, their use being mostly industrial, but in the last few years some diamonds of more than 200 carats have been found. Explored reserves of coal are 4.4 billion tons, of which two-thirds is high quality Neryungri coking coal. In Sakha's one iron-ore deposit located in the republic's southwest, expected reserves exceed 2.5 billion tons.

Sakha also holds the Russian Far East's sole known phosphate deposit (130 million tons of apatite ores, containing 6.7% P_2O_5). Natural gas reserves are estimated at 13 trillion cubic meters, oil reserves are also substantial. Other important resources include tin (good prospects), gold (depleted substantially), polymetal ores, antimony, bismuth, tungsten, mercury and furs. Timber reserves (9 billion cubic meters) are huge, but of low quality.

Prospects

Sakha has been bold in pursuing an independent policy. Control over its resources is the key to its independence. At present it appears to be winning in the struggle for greater autonomy. The failure to complete rail transport into the region (from the Baikal Amur Railroad) will continue to hamper development.

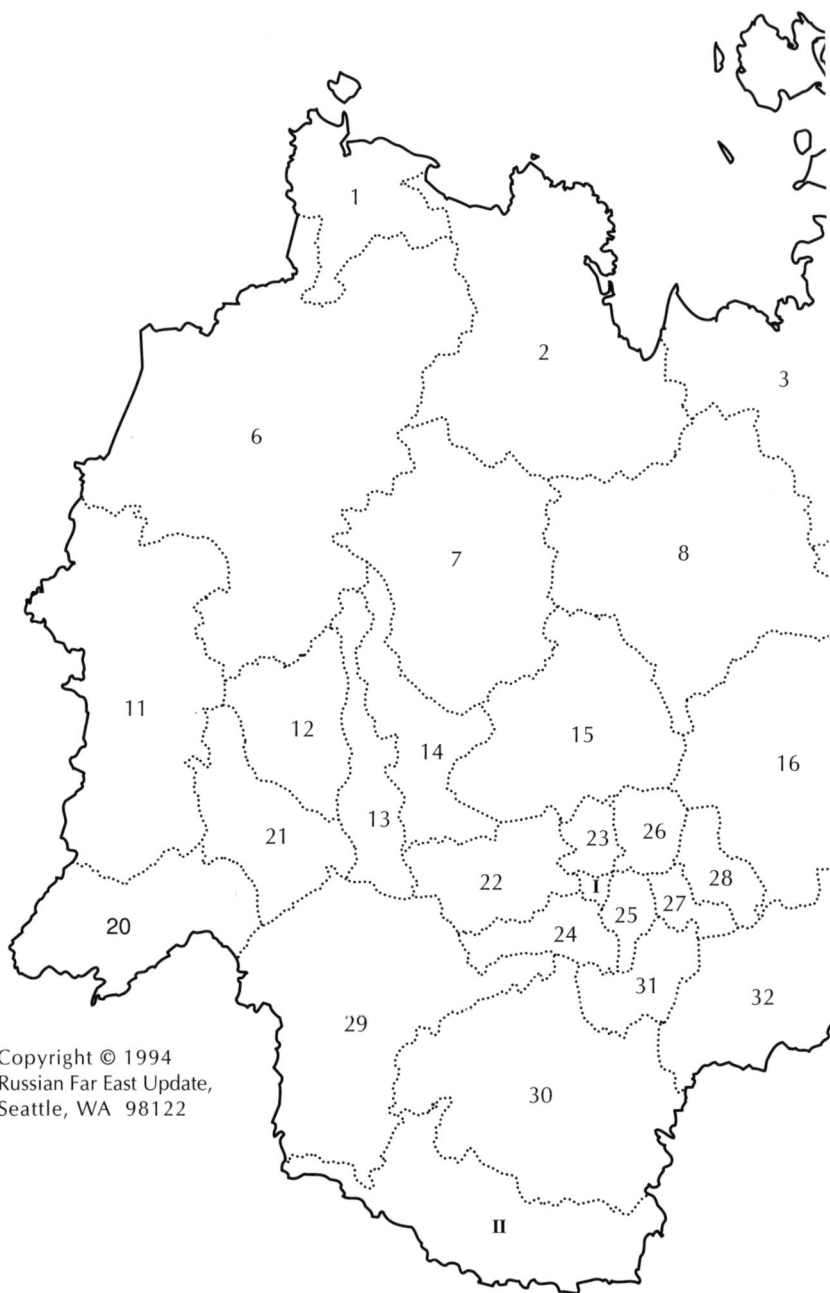

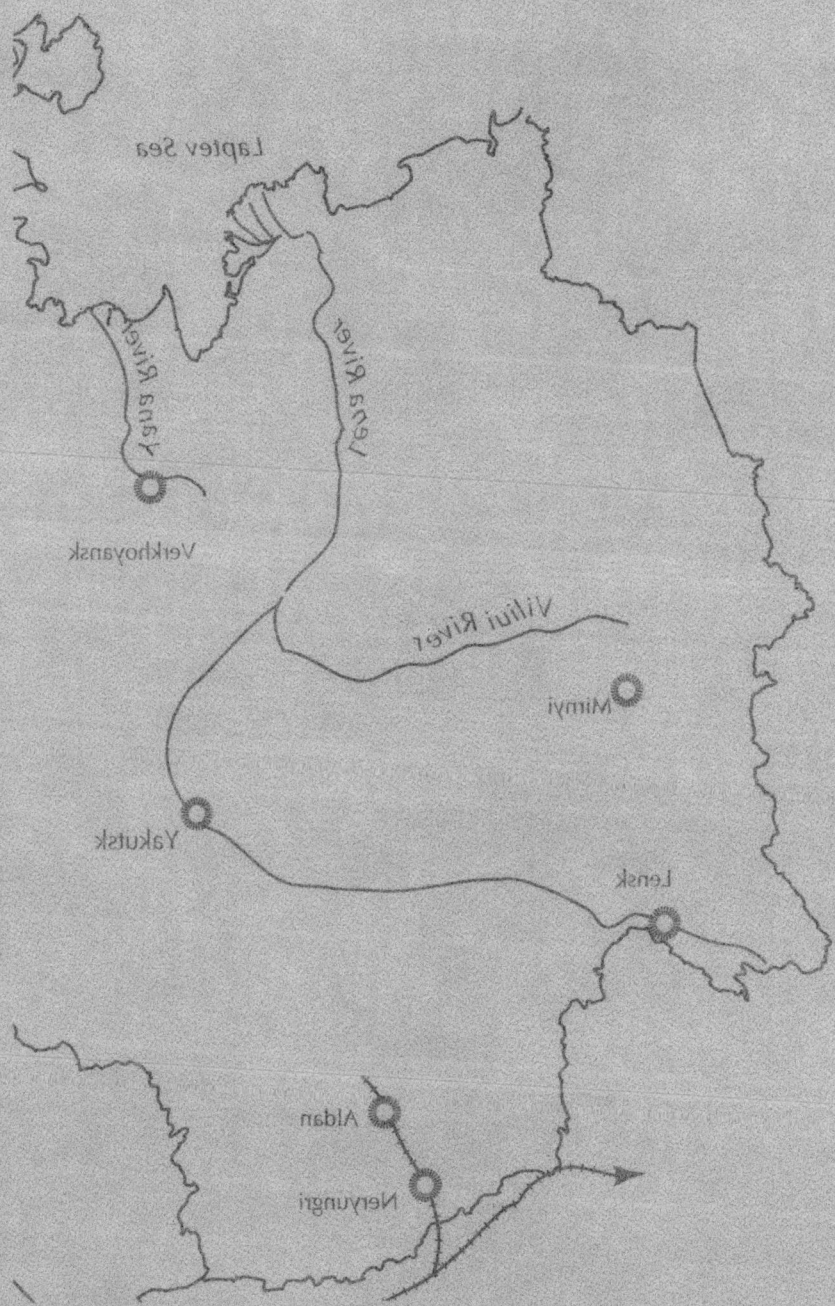

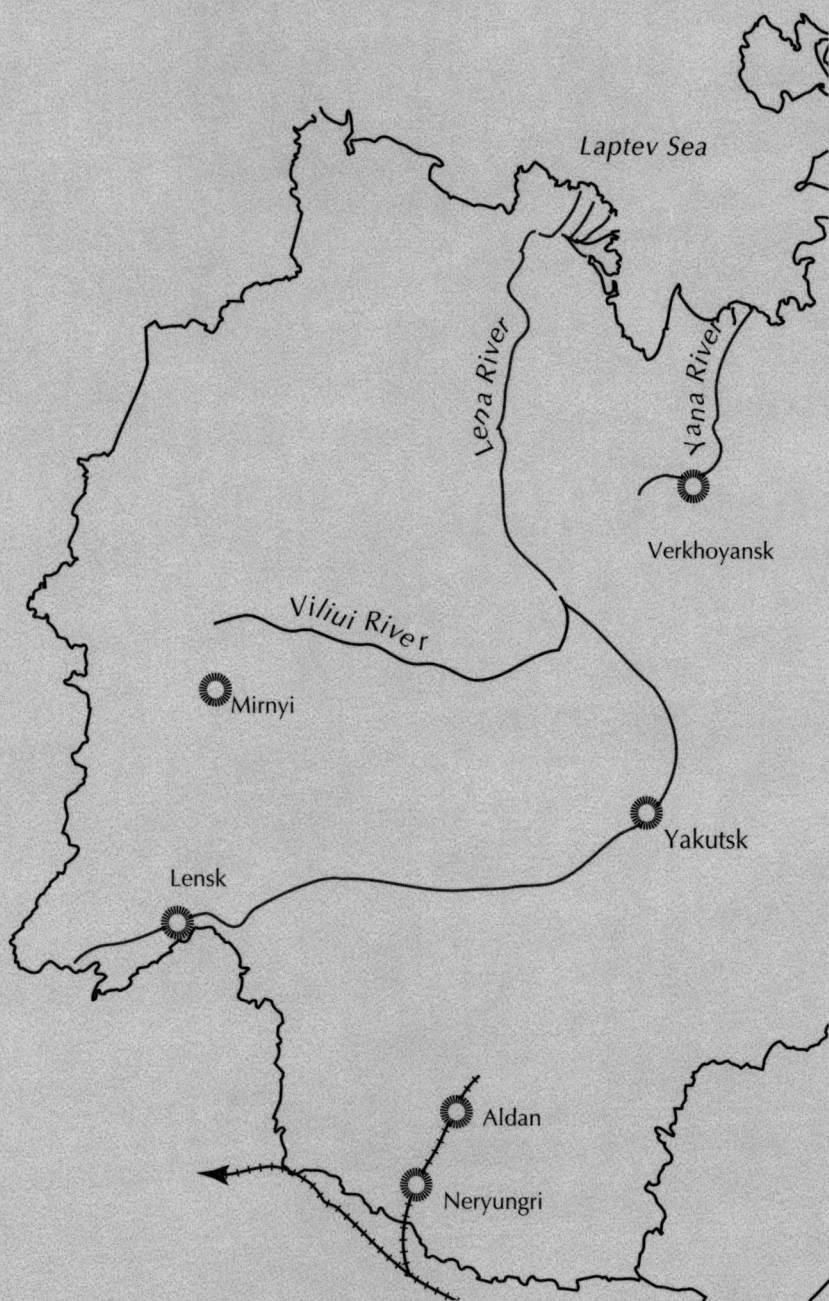

Laptev Sea

Lena River

Yana River

Verkhoyansk

Viliui River

Mirnyi

Yakutsk

Lensk

Aldan

Neryungri

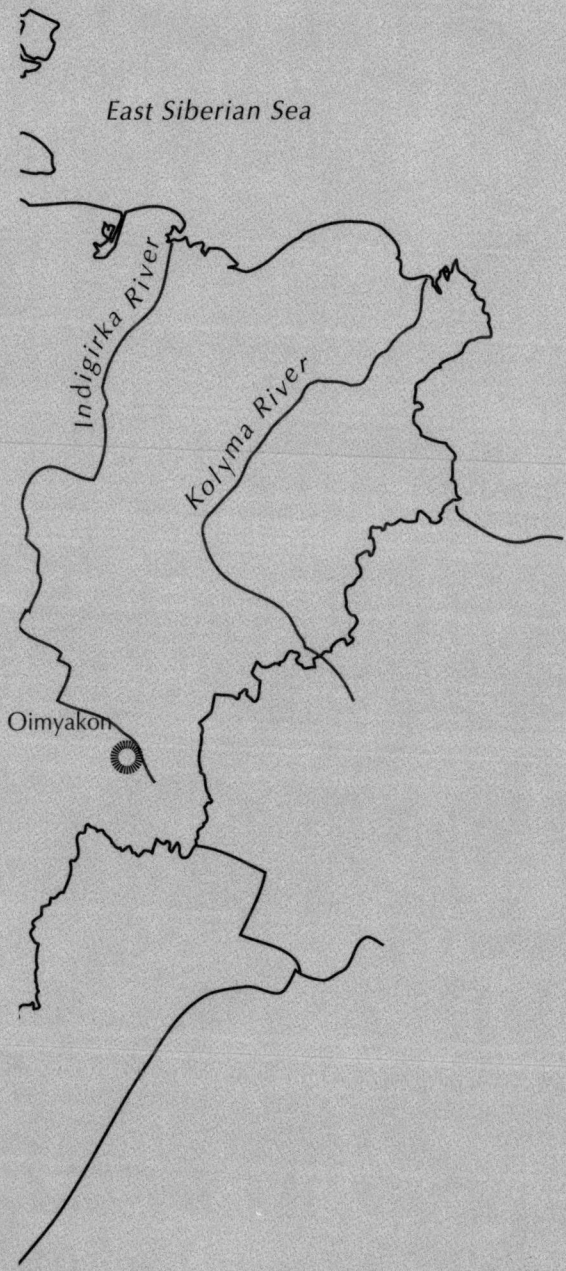

East Siberian Sea

Indigirka River

Kolyma River

Oimyakon

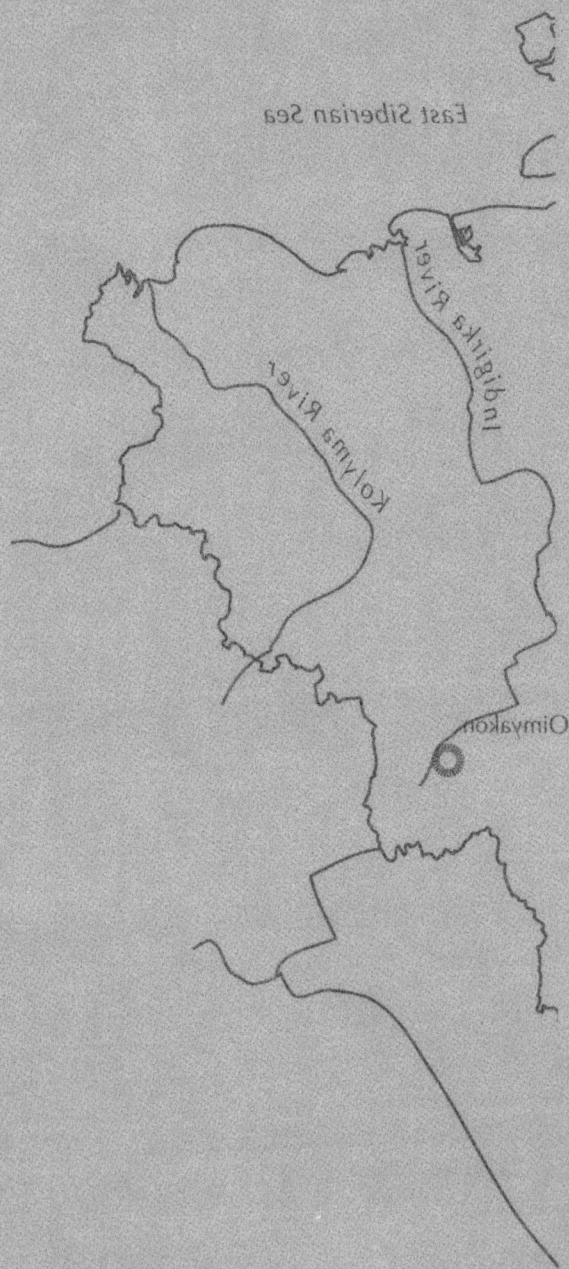

East Siberian Sea

Indigirka River

Kolyma River

Oimyakon

Districts of Republic of Yakutiia-Sakha

Abyiskii	9
Aldanskii	30
Alekseevskii	28
Allaikhovskii	4
Amginskii	31
Anabarskii	1
Bulunskii	2
Churapchinskii	27
Gornyi	22
Kobiaiskii	15
Leninskii	12
Lenskii	20
Megino-Kangalasskii	25
Mirninskii	11
Momskii	17
Namskii	23
Nizhnekolymskii	5
Oimiakonskii	18
Olekminskii	29
Olenekskii	6
Ordzhonikidzevskii	24
Srednekolymskii	10
Suntarskii	21
Tomponskii	16
Ust-Aldanskii	26
Ust-Maiskii	32
Ust Ysanskii	3
Verkhnekolymskii	19
Verkhneviliuiskii	13
Verkhoianskii	8
Viliuiskii	14
Zhiganskii	7

City-Districts

Yakutsk	I
Neriungri	II

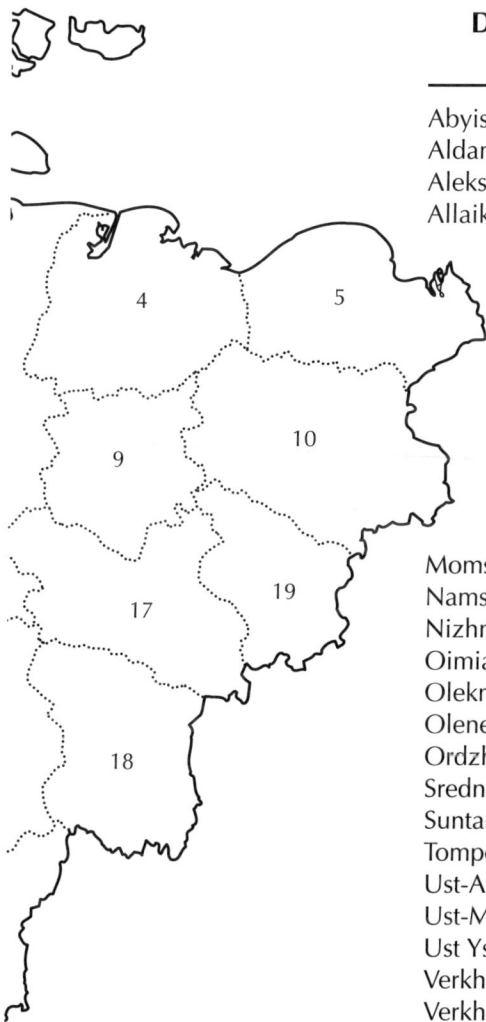

SAKHALIN OBLAST

Population: 713,900
Area (including Kurile Islands):   87,100 sq. km.
Administrative Center: Yuzhno-Sakhalinsk
Governor: Evgenii Krasnoyarov
Telephone: (424-22) 2-14-02
Telex: 213 216 GROM SU

Yuzhno-Sakhalinsk (population: 165,000) was founded in 1881 and ruled by Japan from 1905 to 1945. The city now is a center for light-industry and food-processing. The port of Kholmsk (51,000), terminus for the Sakhalin-Vanino ferry, has two pulp & paper plants, a fishing fleet and a ship-repair yard. Korsakov (45,300) is the island's biggest fishing center; Dolinsk (38,200) and Poronaisk (26,000) head the island's coal and paper industries. Okha (36,800) in the north is the oil & gas center of Sakhalin.

Economy and Industry

Sakhalin's economy is relatively mature and plunged into crisis earlier than other Russian Far East regions: between 1990 and 1993 industrial output decreased by 1/3. The island's economy is based on fish & fish processing, being the third producer in the Russian Far East. Next in importance are timber, pulp and paper. The island produces most of the Russian Far East paper output from seven plants badly in need of reconstruction.

Off-shore oil and gas exploration is a new area of activity: several foreign firms are actively seeking involvement in off-shore drilling. Coal mining annually provides one million tons for export to other Russian Far East regions. Both coal and on-shore oil & gas production are stagnant.

Basic Infrastructure

In the first half of the century, Japanese occupying forces constructed a rail system in the southern half of the island. A domestic airport is located near Yuzhno-Sakhalinsk. The port of Korsakov, on the southern tip of the island, is open to international shipping. The port of Kholmsk is the terminus for the Sakhalin ferry (connecting to Vanino on the Mainland).

Geography and Climate

Sakhalin is surrounded by the Sea of Okhotsk, the Sea of Japan and the Pacific Ocean. The island is mountainous, and experiences strong seismic activity. The two main rivers, the Tym and the Poronai, are located in the northern half of the oblast. Winters are cold and damp, summers are cool and rainy. Fall is often accented by typhoons with hurricane-force winds. Average temperatures range from -13° (8°F) in January to 15° (59°F) in July.

Natural Resources

Sakhalin's proven reserves of off-shore oil are estimated at 1.5 billion barrels of oil; on-shore reserves are almost depleted. Gas reserves also are substantial. Medium-quality coal deposits can support production for many years, but costs are high. Timber reserves are overexploited. The Kurile Islands have substantial reserves of titanium and sulfur; gold also has been found there.

Prospects

Sakhalin is different from the rest of the region. Why?

• Proximity to Japan which makes trade, investment, and travel easier than elsewhere in the region.

• Offshore Oil and Gas: if the billion-dollar deal gets off the ground, the economic effects will be significant.

Districts of Sakhalin Oblast

Aleksandrovsk-Sakhalinskii	3	Poronaiskii	7
Anivskii	12	Severo-Kurilskii	15
Dolinskii	10	Smirnykhovskii	5
Kholmskii	11	Tomarinskii	9
Korsakovskii	14	Tymovskii	4
Kurilskii	16	Uglegorskii	6
Makarovskii	8	Yuzhno-Kurilskii	17
Nevelskii	13	**City-Districts**	
Noglikskii	2	Yuzhno-Sakhalinsk	I
Okhinskii	1		

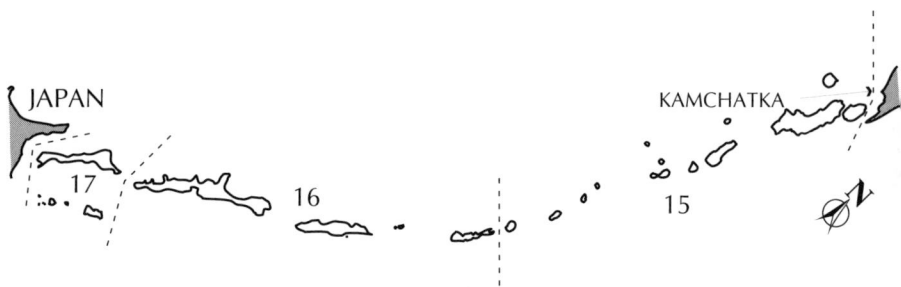

JAPAN   KAMCHATKA

17   16   15

A Bit of History

Oil was first thought to exist in Sakhalin in 1880 when a Nikolaevsk merchant named Ivanov heard Gilyak stories about a 'black lake of death' in northeast Sakhalin where birds perished in an inky mire which they had mistaken for pools of water.....[In the 1890's] Nothern Sakhalin's oil soon attracted international interest. Surveyor Platonov hailed the surface deposits as surpassing those of Baku on the shore of the Caspian Sea. F. Klay, a German geologist, made a detailed survey of the Okha region in 1899. He then formed a syndicate in London ... returned to Sakhalin in 1910 but abandoned further drilling after a year for lack of capital. Meanwhile English and American geologists began to probe the potential of this new Baku. A company financed by German and Chinese capital gained access to oil-rich sites along the Okhotsk coast in 1910. The Russians responded to this interest by forming Petrograd Commercial Association in 1901 (name changed to Sakhalin Oil and Coal Company in 1911 and finally to the Russian Far East Industrial Company in 1914). The Russian Far East Industrial Company included among its directors an assortment of aristocrats, ministers, and Governor Grogoriev of Sakhalin. English capital played a crucial role. Half of the company's shares were held by two syndicates formed in London in 1910.

From ***Sakhalin–A History***
John Stephan

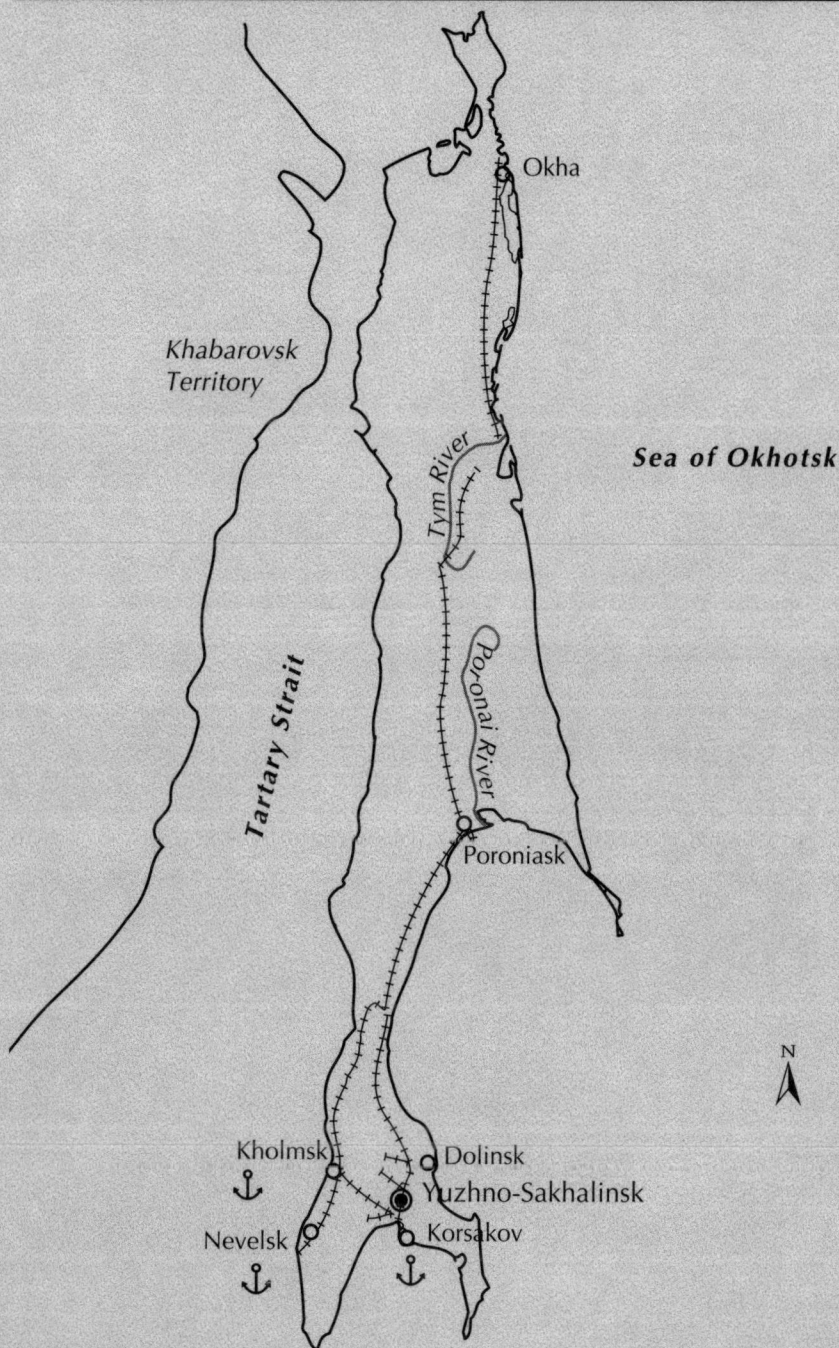

SAKHALIN

Okha

Khabarovsk
Territory

Tym River

Sea of Okhotsk

Tartary Strait

Poronai River

Poroniask

N

Kholmsk

Dolinsk

Yuzhno-Sakhalinsk

Nevelsk

Korsakov

Okha

Khabarovsk
Territory

Sea of Okhotsk

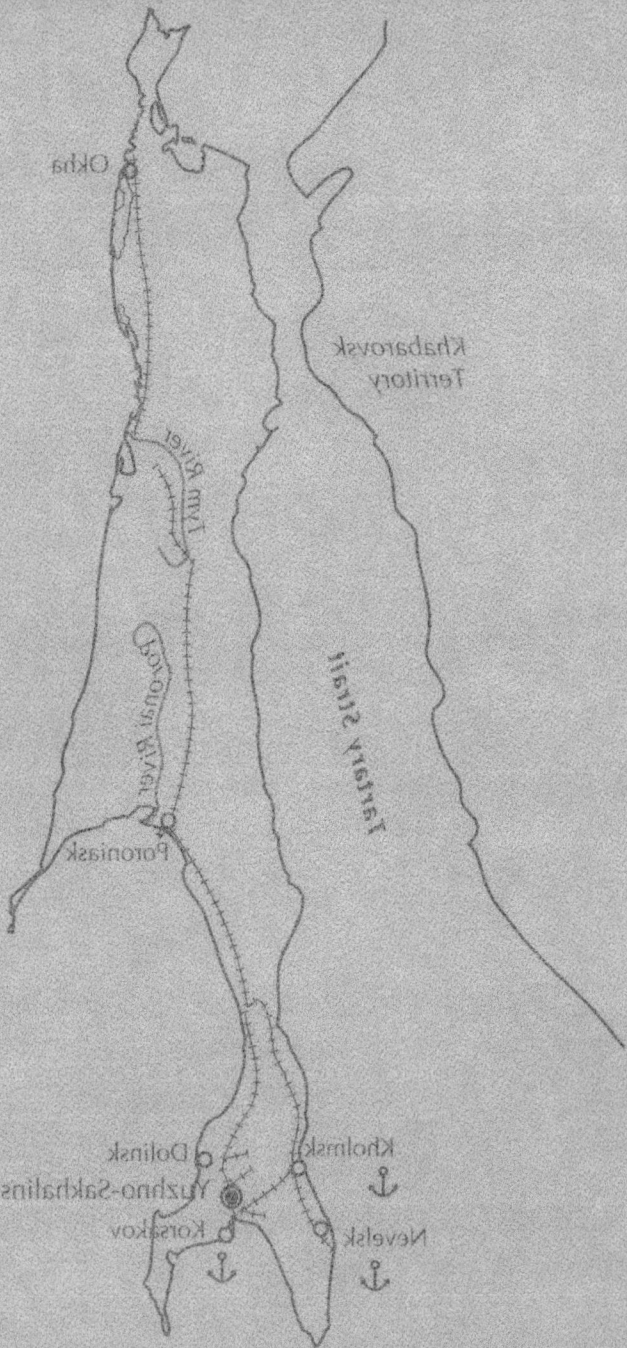

Tym River

Poronai River

Poronaisk

Tartary Strait

Kholmsk

Dolinsk

Yuzhno-Sakhalinsk

Korsakov

Nevelsk

N

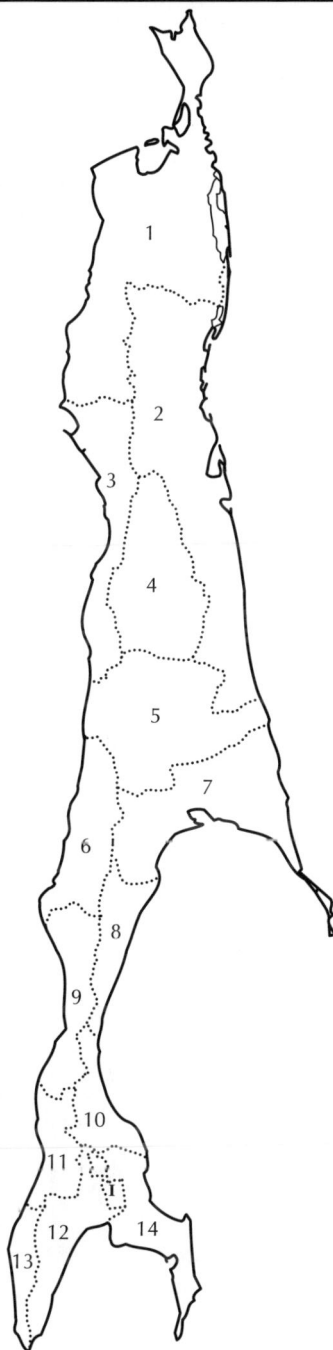

Curtailed or Derailed?
Historical Reflections on Far Eastern Development

John J. Stephan

Wedged between China, Korea, Japan, and the United States, the Russian Far East has emerged as a volatile arena where forces that tore apart the Soviet Union interact with dynamics energizing East Asia. For a while, an outpost of mature socialism seemed to be reinventing itself as the youngest marketable economy in the Pacific Community. Heady perestroikist rhetoric retailed by Gorbachev at Vladivostok in 1986 generated, especially in the West, expectations of engagement and cooperation. But brave new swirls (Alaska-Chukotka "friendship flights") and bracing scenarios (Tumen Delta as a "New Hong Kong") eventually collided with unmanageable human nature. Even before dissolution of the USSR, old networks were reconfiguring under new labels as Party bureaucrats, managers, officers, and chekists took advantage of breathtaking opportunities for self-enrichment. Conducted in an ever-changing legal and institutional setting, jurisdictional squabbles over resources and real estate heightened a pervasive sense of political uncertainty. Shortages and hyperinflation, grist for speculators, played havoc with producers and consumers alike. Entrepreneurial energies increasingly turned to—or accommodated with—crime. "Business" and "profit" came to be identified—by practitioners as well as critics—with philistinism. Hustle, especially if accompanied by telltale signs of affluence, stirred resentment, envy, and xenophobia. Contemplating what a curmudgeon might call a Third World basket case, a more sympathetic observer is bound to echo the question asked by the explorer and traveler Mikhail Ivanovich Venyukov (1832–1901) well over a century ago: "Why hasn't the Amur region[1] developed as quickly and sumptuously as California, New Zealand, South Australia, or even Canada?"

"Why hasn't the Amur Region developed as quickly and sumptuously as California, New Zealand, South Australia, or even Canada?"

*- M.I. Venyukov
1832-1901*

---

[1] "Amur region" *[Amurskii krai]* designated the Far East during the nineteenth century.

Clues that might throw light on this question lurk in the past. Far Eastern history is an elusive quarry camouflaged by exotic languages, skewed testimony, and selective amnesia. Are Russian historians, only partially weaned from official ideology and institutional *kormushki* (feed troughs), ready to discard their blinkers and address Captain Venyukov's question?

Far Eastern development was shaped by both by the state (Imperial Russia, the USSR, Russian Republic) in which it formed a province and by Asia-Pacific neighbors. That duality offers potentials for dynamism and stagnation, cosmopolitanism and insularity. The Far East has oscillated between these two. Historically, St. Petersburg and Moscow kept a sharp eye out for centrifugal tendencies among "colonial" possessions and therefore tended to look askance at unmonitored Far Eastern dealings with the United States, Japan, China, and Korea. To what extent this answers Captain Venyukov's question cannot be said with precision, but a possible connection between proprietary behavior at the Center and anemia on the periphery deserves scrutiny.

Far Eastern development was shaped both by the state in which it formed a province and by Asia-Pacific neighbors. That duality offers potentials for dynamism and stagnation, cosmopolitianism and insularity.

From Ecumene to Outpost

Visualizing the Far East spatially and historically requires a tolerance for ambiguity. Located at the interstices of conventionally defined regions, it straddles parts of the Russian Republic, Northeast Asia, and the North Pacific. At once within and distinct from Siberia, at once connected with and separate from China, Japan, and Korea, the Far East is a matrix of overlapping borderlands. This matrix long served as a meeting ground for diverse peoples and cultures. During the ice ages when water levels fell, the Far East acted as a bridge for migrations between Asia and America. From the first and second centuries A.D., Neolithic communities in the Priamur (lands along the Amur) and the Primorye (Maritime territory) shared affinities with counterparts in China, Korea, Japan, Siberia, and North America.

Starting in the third century, Chinese and Koreans settled the Tumen and Suifen river valleys, heralding a millennium of cultural-political suzerainty in the Priamur, Primorye, and Sakhalin. Korean rule extended into the Khanka Plain until a reunified China under the Tang dynasty destroyed the state of Koguryo in the seventh century. Building a provincial administrative center near what is today Ussuriisk, Tang officials established outposts along the Amur, and collected tribute from native chiefs on Sakhalin. Following the collapse of the Tang dynasty in the tenth century, the Primorye became part of a succession of sinified Jurchen and Mongol kingdoms. In the 13th century, the heirs of Genghis Khan conquered China south of the Great Wall, swept across the Primorye, and—after a long struggle with the ancestors of the Gilyaks and Ainu—occupied Sakhalin. After Mongol rule was overthrown in China in 1368, the Ming dynasty re-established a Han Chinese presence in the Primorye and Priamur. A Ming emperor sent expeditions down the Amur and built a complex of temples on the bluffs of Tyr upstream from Nikolaevsk. The fall of the Ming and establishment of the Manchu Qing dynasty (1644) coincided with the appearance of Cossacks on the Amur.

Starting in the third century, Chinese and Koreans settled the Tumen and Suifen river valleys, heralding a millenium of cultural-political suzerainty in the Priamur, Primorye, and Sakhalin.

Russians represented one of four groups of people converging on territories between Lake Baikal and Kamchatka during the 17th and 18th centuries. "Russian" is something of a misnomer, for the bands crossing Siberia included (among others) Tatars, Poles, Swedes, Lithuanians, and Germans. Meanwhile Chinese, defying Qing prohibitions, slipped through the "Willow Palisade" and Manchu homeland into the Amur Basin. They cultivated crops along the Bureya-Zeya valleys, gathered ginseng in the Sikhote Alin, and grubbed for sea slugs around Haishenwei ("Trepang Bay," now Vladivostok). Koreans crossed the Tumen and harvested kelp along the Primorye coast. Japanese ventured to Sakhalin and the Kurile Islands to fish for herring and trade with the Ainu. "Russian" and East Asian convergences differed in one respect: the former claimed the land and its inhabitants and introduced the notion of state frontiers.

Russian acquisition (some would say assimilation; others–conquest) of the Far East took place over the course of three centuries. Vicissitudes abounded as the quest for furs, provisions, and glory interacted with metropolitan strategies and imperial rivalries. During the 17th century, Cossacks subdued Yakutia, skirted the Sea of Okhotsk, rounded the "Big Nose" (Chukotka), and reconnoitered Kamchatka. Penetration of "Dauria" (as the Russians then called the middle Amur Valley) led to friction with the Qing dynasty whose Manchu rulers could not tolerate intrusions so close to their homeland. After several decades of mutual miscues punctuated by hostilities, Moscow and Beijing concluded the Treaty of Nerchinsk (1689) whereby Russia agreed to withdraw from the Amur Basin in exchange for the right to engage in the caravan trade via Mongolia. During the next hundred years, Russia consolidated its control over the Northeast (Okhotsk seaboard, Kamchatka, Chukotka) and established beachheads in Alaska and the Aleutians. But advances in the North Pacific did not compensate for the loss of fertile lands and of an artery connecting Siberia to the Pacific.

Russian acquistion of the Far East took place over the course of three centuries.

A fortuitous configuration of domestic and international circumstances expedited Russian reoccupation of the Amur Valley in the mid-19th century. Initiated in 1848 by Governor-General of Eastern Siberia Nikolai Muraviev and implemented by military officers, encroachment on Chinese territory had by 1857 left a string of Russian settlements along the Amur and on Sakhalin. Taking advantage of Anglo-French naval operations in the Northwest Pacific before, during, and after the Crimean War (1854–1856), Muraviev secured St. Peterburg's approval for sending expeditions down the Amur to supply Petropavlovsk on Kamchakta. He explained his passage to perturbed Manchu officials as a mutually beneficial precaution to forestall British designs. Meanwhile, his surveyors informed aborigines that they were henceforth subjects of the tsar. Bluster paid off handsomely in 1858 when Muraviev prevailed upon a Manchu prince at Aigun to conclude an agreement defining the Amur left bank as Russian and lands "east of the Ussuri" as a joint possession of the Russian Emperor and Son of Heaven. Interpreting "east of the Ussuri" elastically, Muraviev staked out the Primorye coastline to the Tumen River estuary, thereby forming a common frontier with Korea and cutting off China's access to the Sea of Japan. Weakened by the Taiping Rebellion, distracted by an Anglo-French occupation of Beijing, and ill informed about pertinent geography, Manchu leaders acceded to the offer of a young tsarist envoy to mediate hostilities with England and France in exchange for affixing the imperial seal to the Treaty of Beijing (1860) which, in addition to legitimizing Muraviev's Aigun coup, awarded the Primorye to Russia.

Acquisition of the Priamur and Primorye, together with the sale of Alaska in 1867, established state boundaries on the continent that have endured with minor changes to the present. In contrast, frontiers with Japan oscillated as Sakhalin and the Kurile Islands (or parts of them) periodically changed hands between 1855 and 1945. The notion of a demarcated line forming a state frontier was unfamiliar to China and Japan until Russia irrupted into the Amur Valley, Sakhalin, and the Kuriles. In this sense, the birth of a Russian Far East heralded the death of a Northeast Asian ecumene.

[Russia's] acquisition of the Priamur and Primorye, together with the sale of Alaska in 1867, established state boundaries on the continent that have endured with minor changes to the present.

Imperium vs. Emporium

As early as 1860 it was clear that development of the Priamur and Primorye faced formidable obstacles. Some obstacles—climate, soil, space—were unalterable. Others—shortages of agriculturists, professionals, investment capital, etc.—to a greater or lesser extent could be influenced by government policy and private initiative. But would the state assume responsibility for development? And from where would private initiatives emanate?

Geography placed the Far East in a position to interact with Asian and American neighbors, but geostrategic and political factors determined the tsarist government's approach to the region. St. Petersburg viewed the Far East as a colonial appanage such as the Caucasus or Turkestan rather than as an integral part of Russia. Security concerns about Great

Britain in the 1870s, China in the 1880s and early 1890s, and Japan after 1895 dictated that the region be placed under military rule. In 1884, the Far East was detached from Eastern Siberia and given its first unified regional administration: the Priamur Governor-Generalship. All but the last of eight Priamur governor-generals were army officers, each with broad executive and judicial powers.

For all their prerogatives within the region, Priamur governor-generals carried little weight in metropolitan deliberations about imperial policies toward China, Japan, and Korea. They could do nothing to halt a hapless venture into Manchuria and Korea that started with the Triple Intervention against Japan in 1895 and ended ignominiously in defeat by Japan in 1904-5. St. Petersburg disregarded warnings by one Priamur governor-general against getting involved in Korea and brushed aside pleas by another to build a railroad to Vladivostok on Russian territory along the Amur rather than across Manchuria. The latter option—the Chinese Eastern Railroad—was chosen, giving birth to what has been aptly called "the damned inheritance" that chronically plagued tsarist and Soviet governments. Russia's adventure in Manchuria damaged Far Eastern development by diverting metropolitan capital and energies from Khabarovsk and Vladivostok to Harbin and Dairen, the latter (while under Japanese rule) draining off the bulk of trans-continental freight and passenger traffic from 1905 until the Second World War.

Security concerns ... dictated that the region be placed under military rule.

Priamur governor-generals varied in their views toward regional development. As army generals (save the last), they saw development in terms of military needs. The Imperial Army and Navy were major consumer of goods and services, which were paid for by subsidies from St. Petersburg. The more broadminded among them such as Baron Korf made a point of getting to know the region's leading merchants and convoked annual conferences to discuss ways to exploit natural resources while protecting marine life against poachers. All recognized the importance of encouraging *European* (they used the word "white") settlement, a matter directly addressed by imperial decrees (1861, 1882) providing for allocation of lands to Russian and Ukrainian immigrants and the establishment of a South Ussuri Resettlement Office in Vladivostok. They provided for the resettlement of Estonians to start fishing villages around Peter the Great Bay, and they praised the industry and enterprise of religious sectarians around Blagoveshchensk who by the end of the century had made Amur agriculture the most mechanized and productive in the Empire.

Tsarist authorities tolerated foreign commerce in the Far East, but they prohibited foreigners from owning real estate. Some of these restrictions were circumvented by the engagement of Russian partners or by taking Russian citizenship. Massachusetts-born Enoch Emery established a trading firm in 1870 that during the next twenty years introduced Detroit-built river steamers on the Amur. Hamburg merchants Gustav Kunst and Gustav Albers built a network of department stores throughout the Priamur governor-generalship. The Norwegian-American entrepreneur Olaf Swenson almost single-handedly matched the Hudson's Bay Company provisioning Chukotka. Foreigners also gained concessions to exploit particular resources: Tetiukhe lead mines went to a Swiss immigrant (Julius Bryner), the Lena goldfields to a British consortium, Commander Island rookeries to the American firm of Hutchinson & Kohl. Japanese, thanks to the Treaty of St. Petersburg (1875) and Fisheries Convention (1907), enjoyed extensive privileges along the Far Eastern littoral and on the lower Amur River. A French tricolor flew over the Hotel de Louvre in Vladivostok.

Tsarist authorities tolerated foreign commerce in the Far East, but they prohibited foreigners from owning real estate.

In some instances authorities resisted foreign involvement. In the late 1850s St. Petersburg vetoed American proposals to handle Amur Valley commerce and build a Baikal-Amur Railroad, and in the 1870s did the same to an American bid to mine Sakhalin coal deposits. Americans were unsuccessful in taking part in construction of the Ussuri Railroad during the 1890s and early 1900s. Russian Jewish émigrés setting up businesses as naturalized U.S. citizens found themselves unwelcome in certain circles. Connections made a difference of course, judging from a the incidence of aristocratic and military titles among Russian partners of foreign concessionaires.

Lubricating the wheels of development, Russian officials resorted to the venerable practice of *kormlenie* ("feeding", using one's position to help oneself, family, and friends). The Far East turned out to be a first-class *kormushka* ("trough") for those handling access to resources and customers. Experienced businessmen factored *kormlenie* into operating budgets. Vladivostok shipping magnate Heinrich Hugh ("Genrikh Gugovich") Keyserling "fed" so many, that when in 1903 the governor of Kamchatka complained to St. Petersburg about rampant bribery, the minister of interior ordered the poor man to a lunatic asylum. Olaf Swenson navigated his Chukotka trading company through revolution, civil war, and sovietization by outfitting local authorities with boots, mackinaws, and Winchesters. A 1914 British guidebook matter-of-factly advised trans-Siberian passengers to be prepared for the "Russian genius for squeeze." Unfortunately for Far Eastern development, quite a few businessmen and travelers went elsewhere rather than submit to being mulcted.

For most of the years between 1862 and 1917, the Far East was a free trade zone. Smuggling went hand in hand with graft...

Smuggling went hand in hand with graft, nourished by vendable resources, voracious demand for certain consumer goods, and porous frontiers. For most of the years between 1862 and 1917, the Far East was a free trade zone. Contraband flourished largely because of state regulation of gold sales and heavy duties on alcohol and tobacco. Bibulous Cossacks found it unreasonable not to take advantage of the proximity of Manchurian distilleries. In a seasonal burst of piety, Blagoveschensk-area Cossacks joined Molokans crossing the Amur and celebrated Epihany in Heihe. They returned lustily chanting hymns and carrying buckets of "holy water." Chinese grew opium poppies in full view of South Ussuri constabularies. Nearly half of the ore extracted from the Amur goldfields between 1890 and 1916 was smuggled into China, often in imaginative ways. At least one "sleeping baby" cuddled by a border-crossing mother turned out to be a nugget-stuffed corpse.

Smuggling reinforced negative images of local East Asians (colloquially called "Yellows"). Chinese dominated retail food markets and made up the overwhelming majority of workers in the Amur goldfields, on Amur Railroad construction sites, and in Vladivostok shipyards. Koreans, well over the 64,000 officially registered in 1914, played a crucial economic role in the southern Primorye, where many were tenant farmers for Russian and Ukrainian landlords. Chinese tended to stay apart, but Koreans, especially the younger generation, showed greater readiness to assimilate. Some adopted the Orthodox faith. Their energy and perspicacity won admirers but also elicited epithets such as "Yellow Yids." Suspicion of East Asian minorities mounted after the war of 1904-5, when it became apparent that elements of the local Japanese community (photographers, priests, and prostitutes) had served as intelligence agents and that local Chinese had welcomed Japan's victories. The last two Priamur governor-generals considered massive deportation of Chinese but were constrained by opposition in St. Petersburg and by the non-cooperation of mine owners.

The final decades of tsarist rule in the Far East reverberated with analogies. Expressions such as "New America" and "Amur California" greeted the ear. A Chinese traveler affirmed that Vladivostok would someday become a Northern Shanghai. In 1909, former army minister Aleksei Kuropatkin predicted that by the year 2000 no less than 100,000,000 Russians would be living on the Pacific. The 1913 Romanov tricentennial was celebrated by an Agricultural Exhibition at Khabarovsk attended by the Norwegian explorer Fridtjof Nansen, who agreed with local officials that the Priamur faced a radiant future. A railroad bridge across the Amur, fulfilling the dream of a trans-Siberian line entirely on Russian soil, was completed just in time (October 1916) to serve as a lightning rod for revolution.

One of Russia's few gateways to the outside world ... Vladivostok blossomed into one of the most cosmopolitan ports in Northeast Asia, a unique blend of Siberia, Shanghai, and Wild West.

Regionalist Impulse

War, civil war, and revolution (1914–1922) internationalized the Far East as never before. One of Russia's few gateways to the outside world thanks to a blockade by the Central Powers, Vladivostok blossomed into one of the most cosmopolitan ports in Northeast Asia, a unique blend of Siberia, Shanghai, and Wild West. A dozen languages reverberated in the lobby of the Versailles Hotel. A dozen currencies circulated, including U.S. dollars, Chinese yuan, Japanese yen, Japanese military script, Japanese company script (one merchant printed money bearing his own portrait), Kunst & Albers vouchers, and seven types of rubles: Tsarist, Kerensky, Soviet, Horvath, Kolchak, Zemstvo, Semyonov, and Socialist Revolutionary. Kiosks sold New York, Tokyo, and London newspapers as well as Monarchist, Menshevik, and Bolshevik dailies. Chinese guilds and Japanese trading houses rubbed shoulders with the National City Bank, International Harvester, the YMCA, the Knights of Columbus, and the American Red Cross. Almost everyone who was anyone turned up at one time or another at the Chicago Cafe, although a transient named Somerset Maugham only had time for cabbage soup and a shot of vodka at the station restaurant.

Cut off from Moscow, Far Easterners grew accustomed to fending for themselves.

Moscow at this time used the Far East for larger political objectives. Lenin personally sanctioned a 60-year leasehold of Kolyma and Kamchakta to a Hollywood impresario (mistaking him for a member of a banking family with whom he happened to share a surname). Northern Sakhalin almost came on the auction bloc for $1 billion. Sinclair Oil was given a concession on Sakhalin. Lenin engineered the establishment of a nominally independent regional buffer state (the Far Eastern Republic or FER) to expedite the withdrawal of Japan's expeditionary forces from Transbaikalia, the Priamur, and Primorye.

These maneuvers achieved their international objectives but at the same time promoted skepticism and self-reliance within the Far East. Cut off from Moscow, Far Easterners grew accustomed to fending for themselves. Intended to serve as a fig leaf for a metropolitan game plan, the FER turned out to be a catalyst for regional consciousness.

Dissolution of the FER in November 1922 did not change matters that much, for most of the "Soviet" Far East remained outside of Moscow's control. Japanese troops occupied northern Sakhalin, and anti-Communist nationalism percolated in Yakutia. Peasants and Cossacks resisted grain requisitions. Perhaps because the United States Geodetic Expedition had recently surveyed the coast of Chukotka, leaving behind bronze markers with the inscription: "$250 fine for removal," some Chukchi gained the impression that their homeland had been sold to the Americans. Protected by the Imperial Navy, Japanese landed at will and helped themselves to fish and crab. Frontiers existed only on paper. Chukchi and Koreans moved back and forth across the Bering Straits and Tumen River respectively. In 1928, Gatsbys cruising the Pacific on a Rockefeller family yacht called at Uelen without bothering to inform Soviet authorities. Manchurian bandits and White bands forayed into the Priamur and Primorye. Two thirds of gold extracted from the Amur fields wound up in China. Smugglers supplied inland settlements with guns, clothing, kitchenware, farm implements, not to mention alcohol (stowed in locomotive boilers). News reached remote areas belatedly. When a Soviet patrol boat called at Provideniya in 1924, a local policeman came aboard to arrest captain and crew for flying a red flag.

News reached remote areas belatedly. When a Soviet patrol boat called at Provideniya in 1924, a local policeman came aboard to arrest captain and crew for flying a red flag.

All this meant that the Far East was for much of the 1920s on its own economically. Moscow could spare neither capital nor cadres, so the task of reconstruction fell upon regional authorities who had little choice but to rely on foreign capital, private enterprise, and "bourgeois experts."

Thrust back upon their own resources, a cohort of former FER officials and veterans of the civil war set about rebuilding the Far East (Priamur governor-generalship boundaries were retained), enlisting the services of pre-revolutionary firms (Bryner & Co., Swenson, Bank of Korea, etc.) and seeking capital investments and technology in exchange for exports of fish and timber to China and Japan. Regional authorities considered encouragement of Korean and Japanese immigration to develop a rice industry on the Khanka Plain. The results of these ideas are difficult to measure because the efforts themselves were cut short during 1928–32 when the First Five-Year Plan and forced collectivization pushed the Far East into a lock-step march with other parts of the USSR.

Unhealed Wounds

The rise of international tensions after Japan's seizure of Manchuria interacted with Stalinism to derail Far Eastern development from its regionalist-cosmopolitan trajectory. Development for the next half century was subsumed to metropolitan agendas. Cut off from the outside world except for Moscow-sanctioned, closely monitored links, the Far East transformed into a beneficiary of state subsidies (to maintain large military and border guard deployments) and a provider of raw materials. An illusion of progress was maintained by apocalyptic targets and giant projects (BAM, Kolyma, Komsomolsk), confirming the wisdom of William Gerhardie's[2] remark that "there is nothing petty in the Russian mind when it comes to the gap between the scale of conception and the amount of achievement."

Cut off from the outside world ...the Far East transformed into a beneficiary of state subsidies and a provider of raw materials.

The command economy was only one wheel of a juggernaut that wrought damage from which the Far East has yet to recover. Stalinism "from above" and "from below" destroyed the Far East's most productive agriculturists, exiling religious sectarians, deporting Chinese, and forcibly relocating Koreans to Central Asia. Convinced of a secessionist conspiracy involving Red Army commanders, Old Bolsheviks, Far Eastern elites, and Japanese militarists, Stalin and his security henchmen annihilated not just the prerevolutionary intelligentsia (or what was left of it after the exodus of 1918–22) but also those in all walks of life who had worked for the Far East's participation in Asia-Pacific markets. To preclude any recrudescence of a regionalist challenge, Stalin and his successors balkanized the Far East, carving what had since 1884 been a single territorial-administrative unit into *oblasts* and *krais* each directly accountable to Moscow. The most terrible consequence, however, was the spiritual inheritance of Stalinism. Like Leninism, Stalinism fostered moral relativism and prioritized expediency, vitiating the individual's sense of personal responsibility for acts committed on behalf of social "progress."

---

[2] Anglo-Russian writer who worked in Vladivostok as an advisor to the British Military Mission in 1918–20.

Real and chimerical Soviet triumphs—victory in the Second World War, growing wheat in virgin lands, the space program, West Siberian oil and gas bonanzas, BAM, and superpower status did little to help the Far East recover from the 1930s. The trauma has been neither exorcized by the rediscovery of a collective memory nor soothed (let alone healed) by perestroikist clichés.

In the last analysis, Mikhail Venyukov's question can no longer be addressed solely by the social sciences, because the answers have taken refuge in philosophy and poetry.

*John J. Stephan is professor of history at the University of Hawaii. His works include **Sakhalin: A History** (Oxford University Press, 1971), **The Kuril Islands: Russo-Japanese Frontier in the Pacific** (Oxford University Press, 1974), and **The Russian Far East: A History** (Stanford University Press, 1994)*

To order John J. Stephan's forthcoming book,
The Russian Far East: A History,
phone Stanford University Press at
415-723-1593.

CHAPTER 3: GOVERNMENT OFFICIALS

In this section we list the Governors of each of the nine administrative territories of the Russian Far East. The Governor (more formerly called Head, Territorial Administration) is appointed by the President of the Russian Federation. All of the Governors presently in position at the time of this writing were appointed by Boris Yeltsin.

As the politics of the Russian Federation are expected to remain rather unstable, we can expect to see changes in these Governors from time to time. Changes in leadership are reported regularly in our newsletter, *Russian Far East Update* (information about which is located at the end of this Handbook).

Governors

Amur Oblast	Vladimir Polevanov
Chukotka Autonomous Okrug	Alexander V. Nazarov
Jewish Autonomous Oblast	Nikolai Volkov
Kamchatka Oblast	Vladimir A. Biryukov
Khabarovsk Krai	Victor I. Ishaev
Magadan Oblast	Victor G. Mikhailov
Primorskii Krai	Evgenii Nazdratenko
Republic of Sakha	Nikhail Nikolaev (President)
Sakhalin Oblast	Evgenii Krasnoyarov

Besides the Governor of each territory, there is a local legislature or council, which also (in theory at least) has significant powers. In October 1993 Yeltsin disbanded the National Parliament. Later, he did the same for the local legislative councils. Elections were called to form new councils, renamed the local *duma*, for each of the territories.

Although elections for the local dumas were held in early 1994, most of the new dumas do not have all their seats filled; in some territories, elections were postponed entirely. Formerly the Governor and the legislative councils could be considered to be two bases of power; we can expect this situation to reestablish itself in the near future.

We do not list here elected members of the local legislative councils because of the incompleteness of the election results in some instances and because of the postponement of elections in other instances.

Members elected from the Russian Far East to the Federal Assembly are listed on the following pages. There are two chambers to the Federal Assembly: The Council of the Federation (Upper Chamber) and the Duma (the Lower Chamber). Several of the Russian Far East Governors are also members of the Upper Chamber.

Elected Members of the Federal Assembly from the Russian Far East

Council of the Federation (Upper House)

Amur Oblast

Leonid Victorovich Korotkov
Born: 1965
Nationality: Russian
Party: Communist Party of Russia
Occupation: Editorial Director, newspaper
Amurskaia Pravda
Residence: Blagoveshchensk

Pavel Semenovich Stein
Born: 1951
Nationality: Russian
Party: Communist Party of Russia
Occupation: Unemployed

Chukotka Autonomous Okrug

Maia Ivanovna Ettirintina
Born: 1940
Nationality: Chukchii
Party: Independent
Occupation: Unemployed

Ludmila Stepanovna Kotesova
Born: 1947
Nationality: Russian
Party: Russia's Choice
Occupation: Director, Legal Department,
Chukotka Autonomous Okrug
Residence: Anadyr

Jewish Autonomous Oblast

Gennadii Alekseievich Antonov
Born: 1949
Nationality: Russian

Party: Socialist Workers Party
Occupation: Deputy Chairman, Council of
Peoples' Deputies for the Jewish Autonomous
Oblast
Residence: Birobidzhan

Nikolai Mikhailovich Volkov
Born: 1951
Nationality: Russian
Party: Independent
Occupation: Governor, Jewish Autonomous
Oblast
Residence: Birobidzhan

Kamchatka Oblast

Peter Griegorievich Premiak
Born: 1945
Nationality: Russian
Party: Independent
Occupation: Chairman of Kamchatka Oblast
Council of Peoples' Deputies
Residence: Petropavlovsk-Kamchatskii

Ludmila Alekseievna Grigorieva
Born: 1940
Nationality: Russian
Party: Independent
Occupation: Deputy Head, Central
Administration, Central Bank of Russia,
Kamchatka Oblast
Residence: Petropavlovsk-Kamchatskii

Khabarovsk Krai

Viktor Kirsanovich Bulgakov
Born: 1949
Nationality: Russian
Party: Independent
Occupation: Rector, Khabarovsk State Technical
University
Residence: Khabarovsk

Victor Ivanovich Ishaev
Born: 1948
Nationality: Russian
Party: Independent
Occupation: Governor, Khabarovsk Krai
Residence: Khabarovsk

Koriak Autonomous Okrug

Sergei Gennadievich Leushkin
Born: 1950
Nationality: Russian
Party: Independent
Occupation: Chief Administrator, Koriak
Autonomous Okrug
Residence: Palana

Grigorii Mikhailovich Oinvid
Born: 1960
Nationality: Koriak
Party: Independent
Occupation: President's Representative to the
Koriakskii Autonomous Okrug
Residence: Palana

Magadan Oblast

Mikhail Aleksandrovich Shliapin
Born: 1944
Nationality: Russian
Party: Independent
Occupation: Head, Magadanagropromstroi
Residence: Magadan

Valentin Ivanovich Svetkov
Born: 1948
Nationality: Russian
Party: Independent
Occupation: General Director, Magadanneiud
Residence: Magadan

Primorskii Krai

Evdokia Aleksandrovna Gayer
Born: 1934
Nationality: Nanai
Party: Russia's Choice
Occupation: Deputy Head, Russian State
Committee for Socio-Economic Development of
the North
Residence: Moscow

Evgenii Ivanovich Nazdratenko
Born: 1949
Nationality: Russian
Party: Independent
Occupation: Governor, Primorskii Krai
Residence: Vladivostok

Sakhalin Oblast

Mikhail Aleksandrovich Romanovskii
Born: 1947
Nationality: Russian
Party: Independent
Occupation: General Director, Sakhalin
Shipping Company
Residence: Kholmsk

Evgenii Alekseievich Krasnoyarov
Born: 1939
Nationality: Russian
Party: Independent
Occupation: Governor, Sakhalin Oblast
Residence: Yuzhno-Sakhalinsk

Federal Duma (Lower House)

Amur Oblast

Andrei Aleksandrovich Zakharov
Born: 1961
Nationality: Russian
Party: Independent
Occupation: Teacher, Polytechnical Institute
Residence: Blagoveshchensk

Chukotka Autonomous Okrug
Tatiana Gennadievna Nesterenko
Born: 1959
Nationality: Russian
Party: Independent
Occupation: Chief Administrator of Finance,
Chukotka Autonomous Okrug
Residence: Anadir

Jewish Autonomous Oblast

Anatolii Mikhailovich Biryukov
Born: 1947
Nationality: Russian
Party: Agrarian Party of Russia
Occupation: Deputy Head, Central Committee of
the Russian Federation Agricultural Workers Trade
Union
Residence: Moscow

Kamchatka Oblast

Ivars Yanovich Lezdinsh
Born: 1952
Nationality: Latvian
Party: Independent
Occupation: Director, Municipalnii Kanal
Residence: Petropavlovsk-Kamchatskii

Khabarovsk Krai (2 seats)

Vladimir Ivanovich Barishev
Born: 1959
Nationality: Russian
Party: Russia's Choice
Occupation: Private Detective
Residence: Komsomolsk-na-Amure

Valerii Borisovich Podmasko
Born: 1958
Nationality: Russian
Party: Independent
Occupation: Deputy Chair, Khabarovsk Krai
Property Fund
Residence: Khabarovsk

Koriaksk Autonomous Okrug

Mikhail Ivanovich Popov
Born: 1942
Nationality: Koriak
Party: Independent
Occupation: Laboratory Director, Koriak Institute
of National Problems of Education, Russian
Ministry of Education
Residence: Palana

Magadan Oblast

Evgenii Mikhailovich Kokorev
Born: 1940
Nationality: Russian
Party: Independent
Occupation: President, International Pedagogical
University
Residence: Magadan

Primorskii Krai (3 seats)

Valerii Ivanovich Nesterenko
Born: 1945
Nationality: Ukrainian
Party: Democratic Party of Russia

Occupation: Director, Khankaiskii Nature
Reserve
Residence: Spassk-Dalnii

Mikhail Konstantinovich Glubokovskii
Born: 1948
Nationality: Russian
Party: Block Yavlinskii-Boldurev-Lukin
Occupation: Laboratory Director, Biological
Institute of the Russian Academy of Science, Far
East Branch
Residence: Vladivostok

Igor Gavrilovich Ustinov
Born: 1935
Nationality: Russian
Party: Independent
Occupation: Chief, Administrative Committee,
Nakhodka Free Economic Zone

Republic of Sakha (Yakutiia)

Yegor Petrovich Zhirkov
Born: 1954
Nationality: Yakut
Party: Independent
Occupation: Minister of Education, Republic of
Sakha
Residence: Yakutsk

Sakhalin Oblast

Boris Nikitovich Tretyak
Born: 1938
Nationality: Ukrainian
Party: Independent
Occupation: Director, Trust
Sakhalingeofizrazvedka
Residence: Okha

Party block seats

Russian Far Easterners occupied only 3 of the 225 seats of the Duma that are allocated to political parties or blocks. These three and their party affiliations are:

Democratic Party of Russia

Yurii Nikolaevich Yakovlev
Born: 1950
Nationality: Russian
Party: Democratic Party of Russia
Occupation: Head of Primorskii Krai Democratic Party of Russia
Residence: Primorskii Krai

Liberal Democratic Party

Evgenii Alexandrovich Bolshakov
Born: 1949
Nationality: Russian
Party: Liberal Democratic Party
Occupation: General Director of AV and AS
Residence: Vladivostok

Political Movement Women of Russia

Svetlana Yurievna Orlova
Born: 1954
Nationality: Russian
Party: Women of Russia
Occupation: General Director, Womens' non-profit organization "Anna"
Residence: Vladivostok

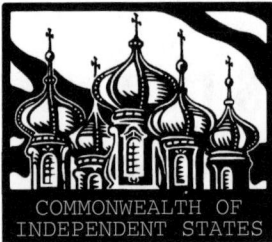

Introduction to Chapters Four through Nine

The material in the following chapters covers a variety of topics on the Russian Far East economy and includes a wide selection of graphs and charts for easy reference. Below we answer two of the questions we are asked most often about our graphs and charts.

What is the source of the data?

The majority of the following tables and graphs use data from the Russian publication ***Russian Far East — An Economic Review*** (*Dalnii Vostok Rossii — Ekonomicheskoe Obozrenie*), published in 1993 in Russian by the Institute of Economic Research (Pavel Minakir, Editor) of the Far Eastern Branch of the Russian Academy of Sciences, which is located in Khabarovsk.

Why does the data not include 1993?

Annual statistics usually become available at the end of the first quarter of the following year. Our publication went to press before April 1994, that is before final 1993 statistics were available. For that reason, for the most part, we represent 1992 as the last year in our tables and graphs.

Statistical updates are published in our newsletter, *Russian Far East Update,* which we issue monthly. (You can find information about the *Update* and an order form at the end of the Handbook).

General. Harsh natural conditions and minimal capital investments characterize today's Russian Far Eastern agriculture, which covers only 15% of local requirements in grain, only 30% of the region's needs for vegetables and 40-50% of meat and milk requirements. Eggs are probably the only staple produced in quantities sufficient to meet local consumption needs.

Foodstuffs represent one of the major imported items for all of the Russian Far East territories. Kamchatka, Magadan and Khabarovsk are most dependent on shipments of food from other areas. It is safe to assume that the Russian Far East will not be self-sufficient in terms of almost any major food product in the foreseeable future.

Diagram 1

Agricultural Output in the Russian Far East

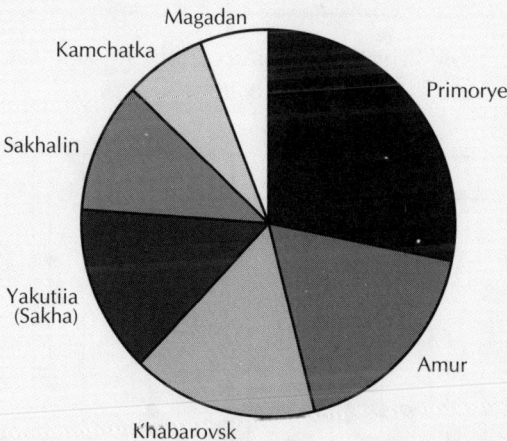

Data are for 1991. Almost 2/3 of the region's agricultural output is produced on the plains of the Amur River valley (in Amur oblast and Khabarovsk krai) and in South Primorye. Primorye and Amur are the region's two major farm producers.

Private vs. State Sector. More than 2,100 large state-supported entities remain the dominant feature of the Russian Far East agrarian sector. Among these enterprises, in 1992, 761 large farms accounted for 90% of all agricultural workers and 3/4 of all farmland. Still, in some areas where reforms are moving faster, the commercial sector is already rather strong. In Primorye the households, farms and other commercial entities produced 38% of total farming output in 1992.

The commercial sector in farming is represented, first of all, by 2.1 million individual households that lease tiny plots of land (pea-patches) near major cities. These private plots produce a noticeable share of Far Eastern farming output. Today, the new commercial private farmer (there were 8,000 farming households at the end of 1992) has-as yet-been unable to make a significant impact on Russian Far East agricultural output. There were 5,000 and 1,850 such households at the end of 1993 in Primorye and Khabarovsk with 15 and 25 hectares per farm allocated to them respectively.

Diagram 2

State and Private Agriculture in the Russian Far East (early 90's)

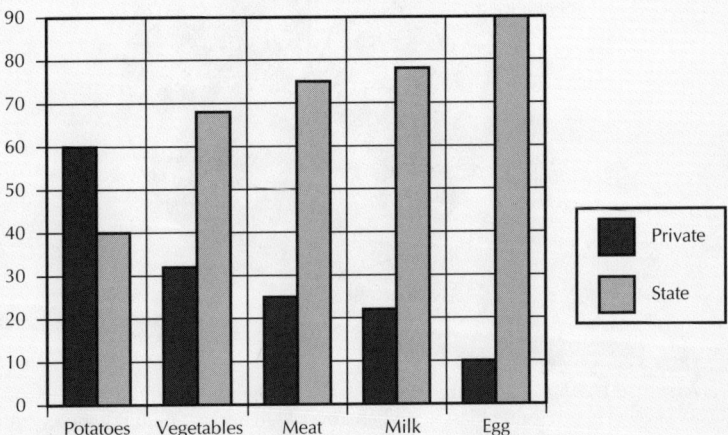

Crises. In 1992 production of meat, milk and eggs in state-supported and collective farms decreased by 20-25% with respect to the previous year.

The crisis in Russian Far East agriculture is related to harsh conditions and a drop in capital investments. In the last decade, according to official data, a 1% increase in farming output required a 20% increase in capital inputs. An increase in farming in the Russian Far East requires capital intensive improvements such as irrigation and drainage. Improved fields account for 12% (824,000 hectares) of total land. At present new important projects have been halted because of lack of funding. Capital investment in farming decreased substantially in 1991 and 1992.

Table 1

Plant Cultivation: Farm Crop Sown Areas   *In Thousand Hectares*

	TOTAL SOWN AREA		CORN		POTATOES		VEGETABLES	
	1980	1990	1980	1990	1980	1990	1980	1990
Yakutiia (Sakha)	99	108	46	24	9	9	1	1
Primorye	764	741	282	229	45	36	16	11
Khabarovsk	284	268	67	62	24	28	10	9
Amur	1,643	1624	736	637	29	26	9	7
Kamchatka	52	65	0	0	6	5	1	1
Magadan	30	37	2	0	2	2	1	1
Sakhalin	43	50	0	0	12	10	3	2
Russian Far East	2,915	2,892	1,133	952	127	116	41	32

Corn harvesting is mostly mechanized. However, most potatoes and vegetables are collected by hand. No wonder that the Russian Far East farm sector, along with the timber and construction industries, employs thousands of "guest" workers (mainly from China).

Farm output. Yield of major crops in the Russian Far East is lower than the Russian average, but private entities are doing better. Undercapitalized and badly equipped individual farms still surpass the state-supported sector in yields of potatoes, vegetables, and milk (per cow).

Primorye is one of Russia's major producers of rice (51,000 tons in 1992). The Amur region accounts for about 80% of Russia's total output of soybeans (323,000 tons in 1992).

Production of honey (mostly in Primorye) is another of the few items produced locally that is significant on the national level.

Low temperatures and widely spread permafrost make it hard to grow crops: as a result, the livestock industry is an important percentage of total agricultural output, contributing 2/3 of total production. The sector is still based on large-scale complexes designed to hold 50-100,000 head of cattle.

Table 2

Harvest of Major Crops   *Thousand tons/year*

	CORN		POTATOES		VEGETABLES	
	1981-85*	1991	1981-85*	1991	1981-85*	1991
Yakutiia (Sakha)	34	22	77	89	29	30
Primorye	303	275	458	349	148	110
Khabarovsk	58	68	272	320	122	76
Amur	566	775	264	328	81	71
Kamchatka	0	0	73	71	24	20
Magadan	1	0	31	23	17	13
Sakhalin	0	0	131	131	48	45
Russian Far East	962	1,140	1,306	1,311	469	364

* Annual mean

Table 3

Farm Yields   *Metric tons per hectare*

	CORN	POTATOES	VEGETABLES	†MILK
Yakutiia (Sakha)	0.8	8.9	17.7	1.7
Primorye	1.3	8.4	7.9	2.0
Khabarovsk	1.3	10.5	7.9	2.2
Amur	1.4	11.8	10.3	2.5
Kamchatka	n/a	12.0	13.0	3.5
Magadan	n/a	9.8	13.0	3.9
Sakhalin	n/a	10.8	19.0	3.9
Russian Far East	12.7	10.0	9.7	2.3

† *1991 Milk yield per cow in metric tons per year*
Data are for 1991.

Table 4

Animal Husbandry   *In thousand head*

	CATTLE		PIGS		POULTRY	
	1981	1991	1981	1991	1981	1991
Yakutiia (Sakha)	394	409	53	112	1,136	1,611
Primorye	433	406	463	364	5,597	6,958
Khabarovsk	203	228	288	392	6,462	6,847
Amur	417	459	346	405	3,765	4,703
Kamchatka	49	63	44	75	1,118	1,604
Magadan	41	47	45	70	1,925	2,289
Sakhalin	85	97	130	186	2,270	2,906
Russian Far East	1,622	1,709	1,369	1,604	22,273	26,917

Introduction

One of the distinct features of freight transportation in the Russian Far East is seasonality. Maximum turnover is registered in May-October, when the Arctic regions are supplied.

The general slowdown in economic activity has caused disruption in the Russian Far East's transport sector. Between 1991 and 1992 total cargo and passenger movements decreased 10-13%, creating idle capacity at some transport nodes. However, there has been an increase in transport carriage on some new routes, especially those which serve Pacific countries.

Railways. The railway system consists of 2 parallel lines: the Trans Siberian (double track) and Baikal-Amur railroads. Both of these are connected by north-south trunk lines. Construction of the Tynda-Tommot-Yakutsk road, 830 km long,

Diagram 1

Russian Far East Ports:
Import/Export Cargo as Percentage of Total Cargo *By weight*

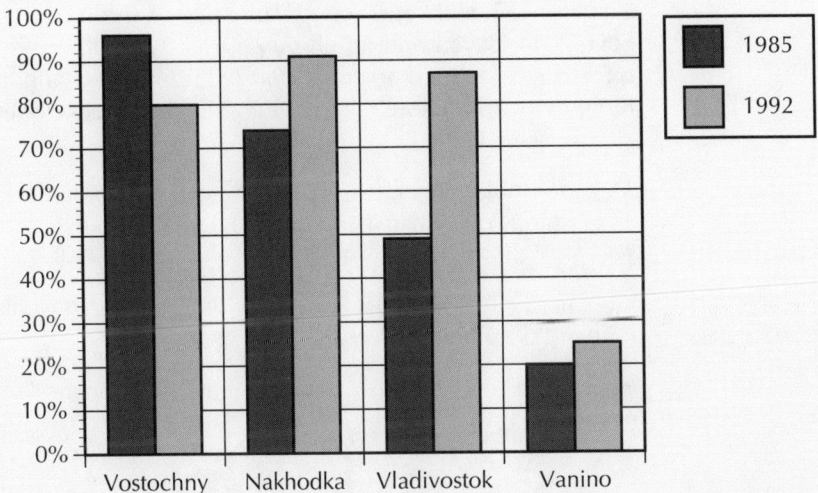

began in 1985 and is complete to Aldan (520 km railroad distance from Yakutsk). The Russian Far East has also a major ferry connection from Vanino (Khabarovsk krai) to Kholmsk (Sakhalin oblast), vital for Sakhalin's economy.

Marine Transport. Russia has 10 shipping companies now, 5 of them in the Russian Far East. All together these 5 Russian Far East shipping companies comprise more than 25% of Russia's cargo fleet. FESCO is a close second (in terms of deadweight) after the Russian Baltic Fleet.

The Russian Far East has about 300 operational ports and mini-ports. Most of them are small and specialize in certain cargo (fish, timber, sometimes minerals and oil). There are, however, about 2 dozen major ports located mainly in Primorye and Sakhalin.

Primorye's major ports include: Vostochny, Nakhodka (Commercial Trading Port, Fishing Port, Fuel Port), Vladivostok (Commercial Trading Port, Fishing Port), Poset, Zarubino, Rudnaia Pristan, Plastun and Ternei.

There are 5 major ports in *Sakhalin* oblast at Kholmsk (Commercial Trading Port and Fishing Port), Korsakov (Commercial Trading Port), Nevelsk (Fishing Port), and Moskalvo in the north, the only specialized fuel port outside Nakhodka.

Khabarovsk krai, in addition to Vanino, has a fishing port in Sovetskaia Gavan and an all-purpose port at Nikolaevsk-on-Amur. A new commercial port (with expected annual turnover of 1.5 ml tons cargo) is currently being developed at Sovetskaia Gavan.

Magadan oblast operates 6 ports: Magadan (Trading Port and Fishing Port), Anadyr, Provideniia, Egvekinotskii, Pevek.

Kamchatka oblast operates 3 ports: Petropavlovsk-Kamchatskii (Commercial Port) and Ust-Kamchatsk (Fishing Port and Commercial Port).

Yakutiia has one port, Tiksi, on its Arctic coast, opened for navigation only 4 months a year.

Diagram 2

Structure of Cargo Traffic by Territory in 1990

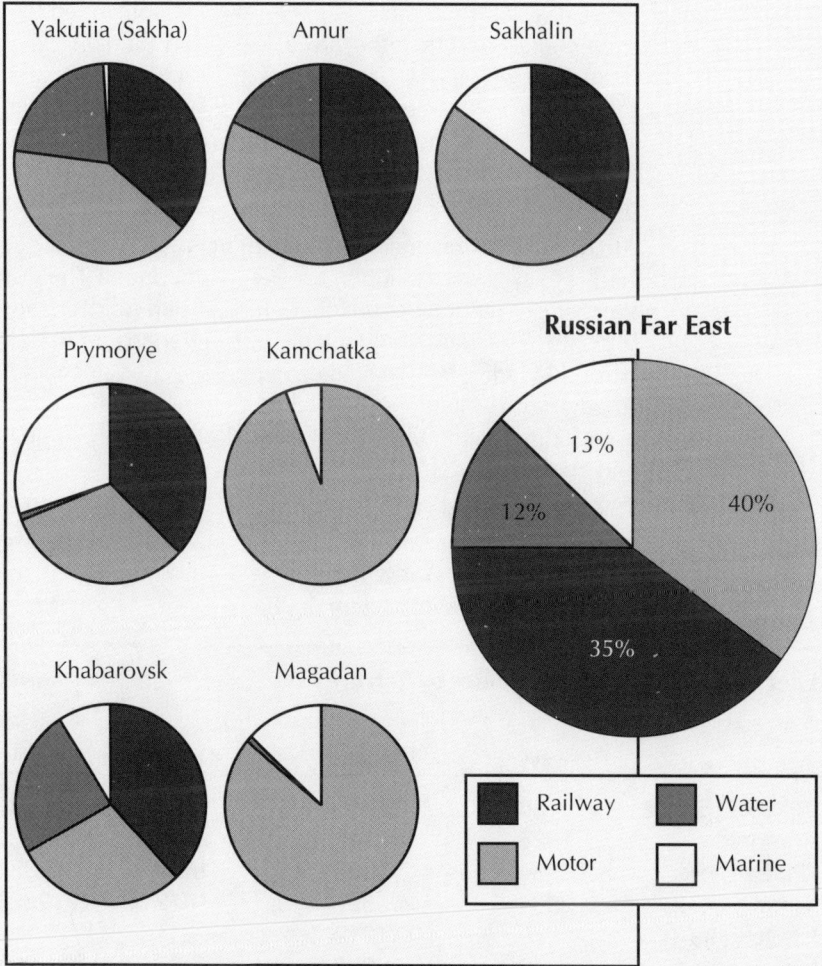

Yakutiia (Sakha)   Amur   Sakhalin

Prymorye   Kamchatka

Russian Far East

13%

12%

40%

35%

Khabarovsk   Magadan

Railway   Water

Motor   Marine

Transit routes. Railway & marine transport facilities serve mainly transit freight. In the Southern part of the Russian Far East, such freight comprises 80% of the total. Russian Far East ports are used for export/import trade not only by producers/consumers in Russia's hinterland, but by many other former Soviet republics as well, for example, Kazakhstan.

River navigation in the Russian Far East is dominated by 2 state-controlled firms: the Amur River and the Lena River Shipping Companies. These companies utilize dry cargo, refrigerator, passenger vessels, and tankers (some of them sea-going). The Amur River Shipping Company serves regular routes to Japan, South Korea and China, and operates a number of joint ventures.

Air Transportation. Inaccessibility of many parts of the Russian Far East makes aviation especially important. The Russian Far East has about 400 functioning airports and airstrips, but only 27 of them could qualify as a regional airport. Khabarovsk, Vladivostok, Magadan, Petropavlovsk-Kamchatskii, Anadyr serve international flights. Other large air centers are Yuzhno-Sakhalinsk, Komsomolsk-on-Amur, Chulman and Tiksi (the latter two in Yakutiia).

The state-controlled Far Eastern Air Corporation (Khabarovsk), the Magadan and Yakutiia Corporations, still dominate the industry. A few independent lines offer cargo and passenger service, mainly on a charter basis.

Table 1

Effective Length of Public Routes by Territory   *in kilometers*

	Railways	Roads*	Improved Roads	Inland Waterways
Yakutiia (Sakha)	156	3549	428	14037
Primorye	1628	7092	2749	133
Khabarovsk	2634	4902	1669	3831
Amur	2984	5697	1512	2635
Kamchatka	0	1212	211	0
Magadan	0	923	297	990
Sakhalin	1069	1857	299	0
Russian Far East	8471	47028	7165	21626

hard-surfaced roads only.

Table 2

Major Russian Far East Shipping Companies

Shipping Companies	Headquarters	Vessels (cargo)	Deadweight (1000 kg)
Far-Eastern	Vladivostok	175	1797
Primorye	Nakhodka	38	435
Sakhalin	Kholmsk	76	378
Kamchatka	Petropavlovsk-Kamchatskii	39	177
Arctic*	Tiksi	23	88
Total		351	2875

Operating in Yakutiia-Sakha.

The number of vessels in five Russian Far East companies decreased from 422 (1990) to 351 (1992) and their deadweight went down by almost 10%, due to ship retirement.

Diagram 3

Russian Far East Ports
Average Annual Turnover in Early 1990's

In million tons

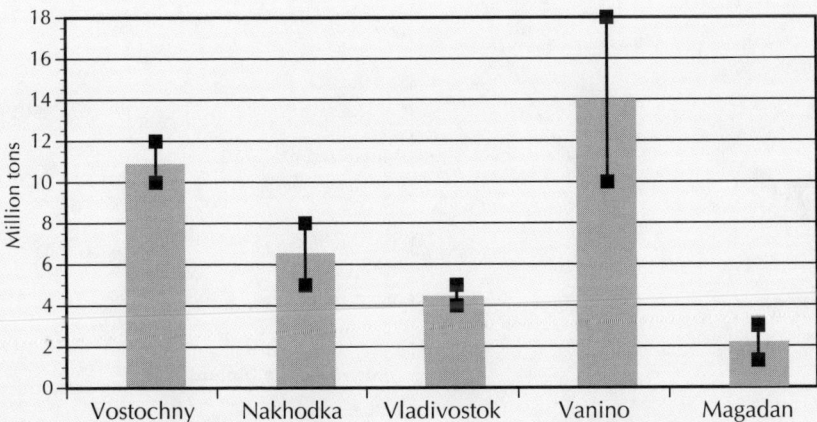

Bars indicate high and low estimates.

WEEKLY SERVICE TO THE RUSSIAN FAR EAST

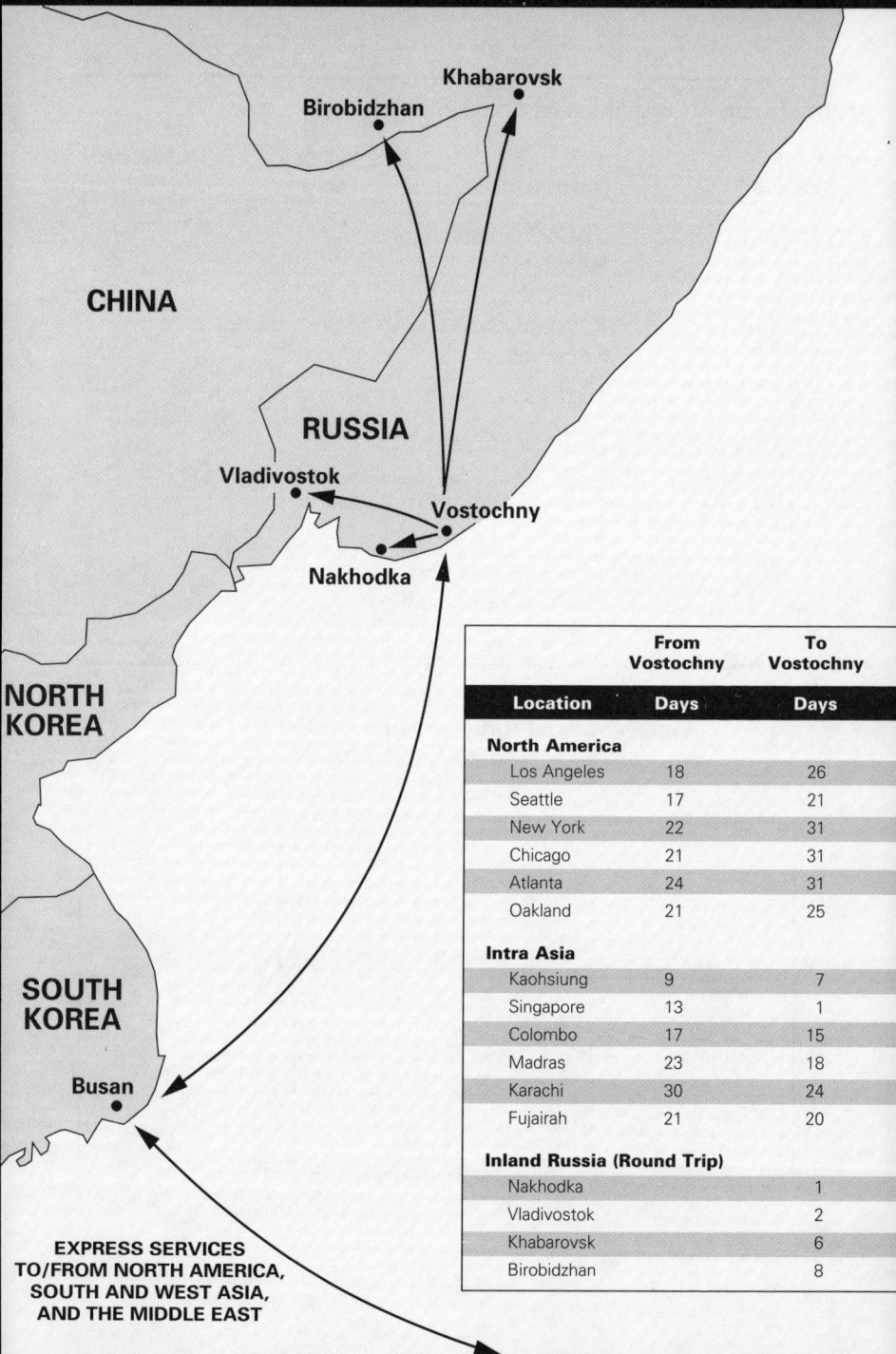

Khabarovsk

Birobidzhan

CHINA

RUSSIA

Vladivostok

Vostochny

Nakhodka

NORTH KOREA

SOUTH KOREA

Busan

EXPRESS SERVICES
TO/FROM NORTH AMERICA,
SOUTH AND WEST ASIA,
AND THE MIDDLE EAST

	From Vostochny	To Vostochny
Location	**Days**	**Days**
North America		
Los Angeles	18	26
Seattle	17	21
New York	22	31
Chicago	21	31
Atlanta	24	31
Oakland	21	25
Intra Asia		
Kaohsiung	9	7
Singapore	13	1
Colombo	17	15
Madras	23	18
Karachi	30	24
Fujairah	21	20
Inland Russia (Round Trip)		
Nakhodka		1
Vladivostok		2
Khabarovsk		6
Birobidzhan		8

PL's weekly service to Eastern Russia offers
the best transit times and most reliable
intermodal service between Eastern Russia
and markets in Asia and North America.
Whether it's refrigerated commercial cargo
or grain from North America, finished consumer products such as electronics and gar-
ments from Asia, or lumber and seafood
products from Eastern Russia, we have the
experience to transport your cargo quickly
and efficiently. With our experienced APL
agents based in the Russian Far East, and
exclusive trucking company based in
Vostochny, we've got the dedicated people
you can depend on to meet your transportation needs.

PL's Eastern Russia operation is an exam-
le of the kind of important, value-added
services that our customers have come to
expect from us. Services that over the past
40 years have included such innovations
trans-Pacific containerships; a variety of
container types; the very latest in informa-
on technologies, such as a 24-hour ship-
ent status and a worldwide internal elec-
onic mail system; and most importantly, a
obal network of transportation experts—
eople who are knowledgeable in the issues
at involve your products and your ship-
ent.

Dedicated Ground Transport

Equipment Versatility

ry 20' and 40' (both low and high cube)
addition to state of the art refrigerated
ntainers are designed to meet your needs.

Thru Bill of Lading

e offer thru B/L's between points in North
merica, Asia, and Eastern Russia.

APL Russia (APL agent)
63 Menzhinskogo Street
Vladivostok, Russia 690600
Tel 7-4232-269-272/339
Fax 7-4232-267-439 or
    7-4232-220-010
Satellite 7-504-915-3131
Tlx 213855 PORT SU

APL Russia/Korea *
14th Floor
Daehan Fire Insurance Building
51-1, Namchang-Dong, Chung-Ku
Seoul 100-060, Korea
CPO Box 6320
Tel 82-2-772-0114
Fax 82-2-753-5056

APL Seattle
3443 West Marginal Way, SW
Seattle, WA 98106
Tel 206-933-4646
Fax 206-933-4612

**APL North America Toll Free
Customer Service Number**
Tel 1-800-999-7733

APL Corporate Headquarters
1111 Broadway
Oakland, CA 94607
Tel 510-272-8000
Fax 510-272-8934

APL Asia Headquarters
World Shipping Center
7 Canton Road
Kowloon, Hong Kong
Tel 852-738-7333
Fax 852-735-1802

*   APL Seoul is the primary contact and
     controlling office for Russia operations.

The Russian Far East and the Outside World

The Russian Far East has always produced export commodities for Russia. In the late 1980s, the Russian Far East produced 40% of the timber exports and 25% of canned fish exports for the former Soviet Union. While the Russian Far East's share of total Russian foreign trade was only 4% in 1992, exports are increasing (in distinction to the trend for the Russian Federation where total trade has been decreasing in recent years). In fact, Russian Far East exports are growing faster than industrial production: recent reports indicate that 8-9% of total Russian Far East output is exported now.

Almost 90% of Russian Far East exports go to Pacific Rim countries. The Russian Far East serves as a gateway for Russia's trade with Asia: 20% of the exports out of the Russian Far East are produced locally, the rest comes from inner Russia.

Japan and China dominate Russian Far East trade.

It's easy to see that in those regions where China is the major trade partner, Japan's role is usually insignificant and vice versa. This feature is not due to some premeditated division of "spheres of influence," but can, probably, be explained in terms of the distinctive features of the local economies.

Japan and China between themselves account for 75% of the Russian Far East trade. Japan's share of trade is significant in three regions: Yakutiia (70%), Magadan (67%) and Khabarovsk (50%). China is the leading trading partner in Primorye (50% of total trade) and Amur (90%). The U.S. has the greatest representation in Khabarovsk (almost 10% of the total trade in 1992).

Forms of trade.

In all the Russian Far East regions, except in Yakutiia with its strategically important diamond industry and in Magadan because of its gold, most export/import trade is conducted by commercial Russian firms, special exporters (authorized by Moscow) and joint ventures. However, the region's foreign trade patterns still reflect agreements and institutions inherited from the trading system of the former USSR: two of these institutions are compensation trade and barter trade.

Compensation trade. In the 1960s and 1970s, the USSR and Japan entered into medium- and long-term contracts which were designed to finance development of Russian Far East natural resources. The Japanese loans were used to develop logging, coal mining, and oil & gas development. In the timber industry, for example, these agreements re-equipped local producers and enabled the industry to generate about 30 million cubic meters of timber exports to Japan over the years which followed. Similarly, the Neryungri coal project

Diagram 1

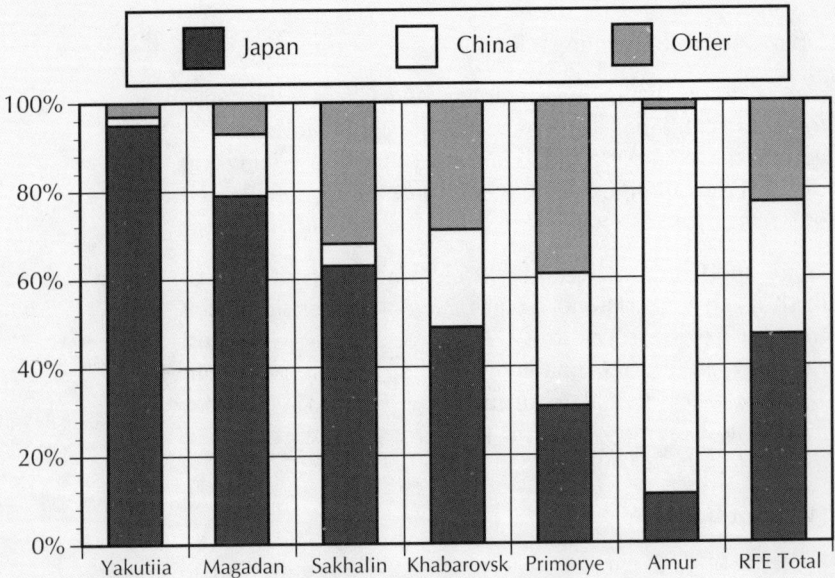

Japan and China in Total Trade of the Russian Far East Territories

Data are for 1992.

(in Southern Yakutiia) received about US$ 1 billion from Japan to secure 5.5 million tons of export annually of coking coal. These agreements are still in force. In another important compensation agreement of the 1970s Japan provided US$ 170 million for exploration of offshore oil & gas Sakhalin deposits (now called the Sakhalin-1 project): again the intent was that output would be exported and the loans paid back.

Barter trade. This specialized trade is carried on with the region's Pacific neighbors, and is another aspect of the Russian Far East trade that began with the planned economy of the former USSR. China is the major Russian Far East partner in barter trade: it controls almost 60% of barter trade operations now. Though barter exchanges are used in trade with Japan and South Korea, barter trade with China is most important. In exchange for consumer goods and foodstuffs from China, the Amur, Khabarovsk and Primorye territories return fertilizer, fish products, rolled steel, and timber.

Trade profiles.

Primorye is in the best position to develop its trade since almost all its transactions are decentralized. Local enterprises managed to get full rights earlier than their counterparts in the other Russian Far East territories. Fish and fish products provide almost 2/3 of total exports.

Table 1

Foreign Trade of the Russian Far East by Territory*			*US$ Thousands*
	Trade Turnover	Export	Import
Primorye	933	352	581
Khabarovsk	497	371	126
Amur	422	232	191
Kamchatka	310	207	103
Yakutiia (Sakha)	213	153	59
Sakhalin	206	137	69
Magadan	141	81	60
Russian Far East	2,722	1,533	1,189

NOTE: * Including trade of joint ventures.
Data are for 1992

Khabarovsk has, probably, the most diversified export structure, sending abroad not only timber, fish and fertilizers, but also military aircraft, vessels, rolled steel and oil products, pulp, copper concentrate, etc.

Amur is rapidly increasing its share in Russian Far East trade. The oblast has an usually high share of machinery in its export trade (73% in 1992). These "machines" are mostly cars and trucks. Amur has almost 500 export/import intermediaries that mainly buy goods in inner Russia and resell them to China. Export/import cargo turnover is greatest at Blagoveschensk (a major locus for trade with China).

Kamchatka is a single-product economy based on fishing and fish processing; it is increasingly relying on foreign trade.

Yakutiia's exports are primarily coal, timber and diamonds. Almost 90% of Sakha's exports go through state-controlled channels. (Diamonds are not included in trade statistics for Yakutiia.) With a very limited number of export commodities Yakutiia has uncertain revenue perspectives. Export of coal decreased 2.5 times to 2.9 million tons between 1990 and 1992 and export of timber went down 4 times. Still, imports in 1992 were 3 times larger than exports because Yakutiia gets back part of the hard-currency proceeds from international diamond sales, enabling local purchases.

Table 2

Major Foreign Trading Partners of the Russian Far East (%)*

	Total Trade	Export	Imports
Japan	35	47	21
China	39	30	50
S. Korea	9	7	12
USA	3	3	2
Vietnam	2	3	1
Other	12	10	14
Total	100	100	100

Data are for 1992.
* Data for Kamchatka are not included here as they were not available.

Sakhalin's timber exports are in decline, but shipments of fish and oil more than offset those losses and now these two items generate 75% of total exports. Currently Sakhalin exports 15% of its total oil production (up from 3% a few years ago). Imports of machinery and equipment for fishing and processing, mostly from Japan, are increasing rapidly.

Magadan has the most isolated economy. Like Yakutiia, its exports are not fully reported. Exports of gold and silver mined in the region are still controlled by Moscow and numbers are not included in statistical summaries. 90% of local trade (excluding gold and silver) is fish products.

Diagram 2

Changing Players in Russian Far East Export Trade

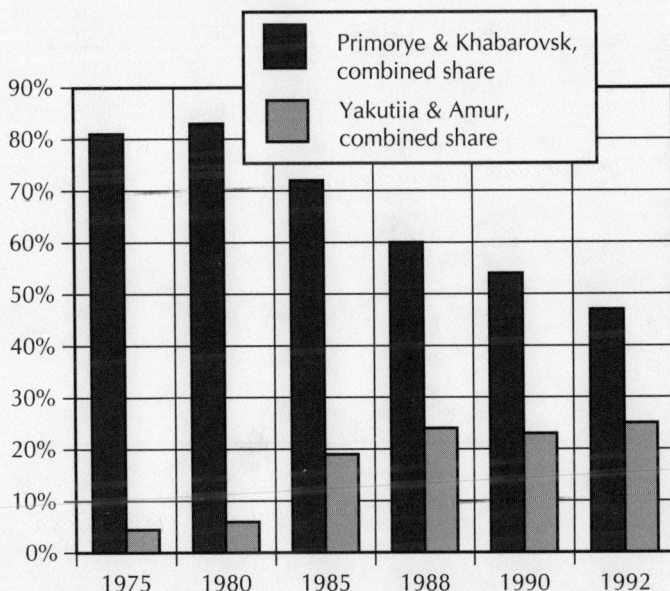

Primorye and Khabarovsk 20 years ago controlled 4/5 of regional exports. Times are changing. Yakutiia and Amur are playing an increasing role. Similarly, the combined exports of Magadan and Kamchatka increased from less than 1% in 1975 to 15% in 1992.

Joint Ventures. Joint ventures on Russian territory become legal in 1988. Between 1988-92, a total of 883 joint ventures were registered. The Russian Far East has incentives most other regions do not offer: a tax holiday of three years for joint ventures registered in the Russian Far East before January 1, 1992 (one year longer than in the rest of Russia). Khabarovsk provided further incentives, giving a two-year tax exemption on profits it collects for joint ventures registered in 1992 and later. Khabarovsk and Sakhalin are probably the only regions in the Russian Far East to provide local incentives. But these incentives are limited: for example, in Khabarovsk, only joint ventures engaged in production (excluding mining and fishing), and where foreign capital contribution is above 30%, are eligible.

Table 3

Directions of Trade for the Russian Far East Territories

Share in the total trade (%)

	Japan	China	S. Korea	USA	Other
Yakutiia	70	5	1	2	21
Primorye	22	46	15	0	17
Khabarovsk	47	23	5	9	16
Amur	7	91	0	0	2
Magadan	62	13	7	6	12
Sakhalin	54	6	18	4	18

Rows add to 100%.
Data are for 1992.

Table 4

Commodity Structure of Russian Far East Exports and Imports*

	Exports	Imports
Foodstuffs	29%	27%
Fuels, Minerals, Metals	27%	2%
Machines & Equipment	18%	24%
Timber & Timber Products	13%	0%
Chemicals	9%	0%
Consumer Goods	0%	42%
Other	4%	5%

Data are for 1992.

*Excluding import/export of joint ventures

Other notes to Table 4:

- The share of consumer goods in imports is under reported because some consumer good items are entered into other categories: cars, for example, a major import, are entered under "Machines & Equipment."

- "Foodstuffs," the major export item, are mostly fish & fish products. The relative importance of this category is also under reported because trade of Russian Far East's joint ventures, very active in fishing, is not included here.

- "Metals" category does not include export of gold and silver. "Machines & Equipment" category does not take into account shipments of arms, manufactured locally. It does include, however, vehicles and other equipment manufactured elsewhere but exported through the Russian Far East. Local commercial firms buy these items from state plants in inner Russia to resell mainly to China. The same is true with respect to "chemicals," which are mostly fertilizers from outside the region exported to China.

- We can also note here that the export of coal, volumes of which peaked in 1990 (at 7 million tons), decreased to 2.9 million tons in 1992. Timber exports, mainly unprocessed goods, also show a significant decline: from 4.8 million cubic meters in 2990 to 1.8 million cubic meters in 1992. Export of crude oil and oil products, however, almost doubled in the same period from 490 thousand tons to almost 730 thousand tons.

Table 5

Export Structure of Russian Far East Territories by Commodity (%)

	Foodstuffs	Fuel, Minerals Metals	Timber & Timber Prod.	Mach. & Equip.	Chemicals
Yakutiia (Sakha)	0	95	3	0	1
Primorye	63	2	1	20	2
Khabarovsk	1	39	32	10	10
Amur	0	6	12	7	73
Kamchatka	94	1	2	0	0
Magadan	90	1	4	0	4
Sakhalin	39	32	14	4	0
Russian Far East	29	27	13	9	18

Data are for 1992.

Table 6

Major Import Items of Russian Far East Territories (%)

	Machines & Equipment	Industrial Consumer Goods	Foodstuffs	Other
Yakutiia (Sakha)*	52	34	1	13
Primorye	11	41	31	17
Khabarovsk	43	29	24	4
Amur	4	64	28	4
Kamchatka	68	6	12	14
Magadan	17	21	11	51
Sakhalin	47	27	24	2

*Including imports of joint ventures. Rows add up to 100. Data are for 1992.

The sizable "other" category for Magadan refers mainly to import of fuel (25 of total). For Sakhalin 1/3 of "Machines & Equipment" ($14 million) are used in fish processing. Construction materials are of some importance for Yakutiia and Primorye, giving about 5 of total import.

Diagram 3

Distribution of Registered Joint Ventures
by Country of Origin of the Foreign Partner

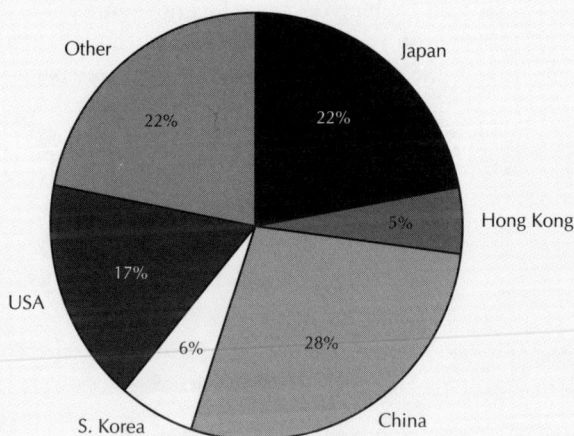

As of January 1, 1993, Japan is still the leader in terms of value of investments in Russian Far East joint ventures. Joint ventures generated almost all of the total trade between USA and the Russian Far East and 3/4 of the trade with South Korea.

Table 7

Joint Ventures: Export, Import, Domestic Ruble and Dollar Sales in 1992

In millions

	Exports (US$)	Imports (US$)	Dollar Sales in Russia	Ruble Sales in Russia
Yakutiia (Sakha)	0.5	3.0	0.6	717
Primorye	78.5	134.5	13.7	1,740
Khabarovsk	97.0	14.3	5.3	2,845
Amur	6.3	5.1	0.0	123
Kamchatka	94.3	22.0	4.5	520
Magadan	16.5	16.2	0.6	103
Sakhalin	93.3	20.5	2.0	960
Russian Far East	387.0	216.0	27.0	5,268

Nakhodka Special Economic Zone. The first law on special economic zones was adopted in 1990, and Nakhodka, one of the early favorites, was explicitly mentioned. Over the years it succeeded in obtaining a preferential status as a special economic zone. However, it is not always possible to tell which declared incentives are really in force for foreign investors and which are just promises made on paper - not honored in reality. At present, the special economic zone offers some, albeit disputed, tax breaks.

The Nakhodka Special Economic Zone is still in an infant status.

Table 8

State Orders versus Decentralized Export (%)

	Exports by State Orders	Decentralized Export	Exports of Joint Ventures*
Yakutiia (Sakha)	87	13	0.4
Primorye	0	100	22
Khabarovsk	12	88	26
Amur	9	91	3
Kamchatka	22	78	69
Magadan	4	96	20
Sakhalin	24	76	45
	Exports by State Orders	Decentralized Export	Exports of Joint Ventures
1988	94.4	6	0
1992	19.3	81	24.3

Exports of JVs are often a major part of decentralized trade. This percentage represents the share of *total* exports accounted for by JVs. Data are for 1992.

Joint ventures now contribute more than 20% of total Russian Far East exports. Joint ventures are often created as an easier way to export raw materials from the region, since they do not need export licenses. That may be why 77% of total export of joint ventures (1992) were fish products, and the rest mainly timber, steel, nonferrous metals and fertilizer.

The majority of registered joint ventures in the Special Economic Zone report their activities as export-import operations, production and trade of consumer goods, car service, transportation, tourism. Nakhodka's Special Economic Zone has a relatively high number of 100% foreign-owned ventures (30% of the total), their average equity being about US$ 0.3 million. Investors come mainly from China and Hong Kong (33% of the total joint ventures), Japan (20%) and USA (12%). In terms of dollar value of the investments, Japanese and US businessmen dominate, with 50% and 25% of the total.

Diagram 4

Export of Joint Ventures from the Russian Far East: by Country of Joint Venture Partner (1992)

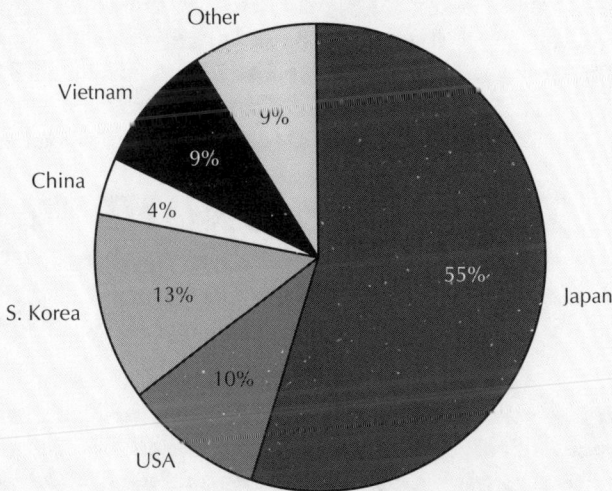

Data are for 1992.

CHAPTER 7:   POPULATION

Population Growth

Until recently the population of the Russian Far East was growing faster than the population of Russia or any other of Russia's regions. This higher than average growth can be attributed in part to higher birth rates. Mostly, however, it has been caused by migration: voluntary migration induced by higher-than-average wages, or involuntary migration (decades during the Soviet era when prisoners were sent to develop the mining regions in Magadan and Chukotka).

Since 1989, however, more people have been leaving the Russian Far East than arriving. Between 1991 and 1993 this factor resulted in overall population decline. This tendency is especially evident in Magadan, where population between 1991 and 1992 decreased by 15%, and in Yakutiia.

Russian Far East birth rates are higher than Russia's average due to the age structure of the population, where reproductive ages dominate. The death rate is lower than average.

Table 1

Population of the Russian Far East Territories   *Thousands, beginning of the year*

	1960	1970	1980	1991	1992	1993
Yakutiia (Sakha)	500	664	863	1,109	1,093	1,074
Primorye	1,375	1,721	1,992	2,300	2,309	2,302
Khabarovsk	1,154	1,345	1,586	1,851	1,855	1,840
Amur	723	793	949	1,074	1,075	1,063
Kamchatka	227	288	385	473	472	457
Magadan	243	352	476	534	509	451
Sakhalin	644	616	660	718	719	714
Russian Far East (Total)	4,866	5,779	6,911	8,058	8,032	7,900

NOTE: Data for 1992 and 1993 are not quite compatible, the drop in population noted is therefore somewhat exaggerated.

Cities and villages. A peculiar feature of the Russian Far East is a much higher than average urbanization rate. In some territories 80-85% of the population resides in cities.

On the other hand only two Russian Far East cities, Vladivostok and Khabarovsk, out of the total of 66 have a population greater than 500,000. According to Russian tradition, the largest city of a territory is usually its administrative center.

Many cities and towns in the Russian Far East are losing population. Depopulation is characteristic and not limited just to mining towns in the North.

Russian Far East villages, and there are almost 3,000 of them, with 650 people in each are, on the average, about 3 times larger than a typical Russian *derevnya*.

Diagram 1

Russian Far East Population: by Territory (1993)

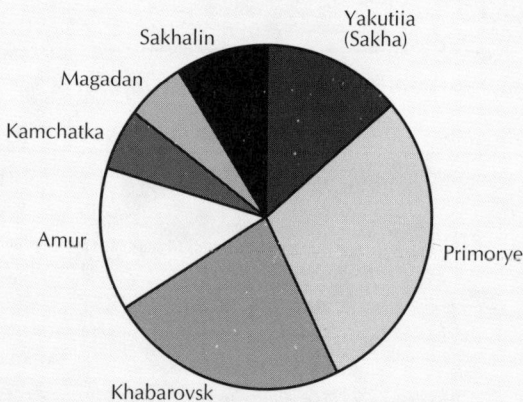

Geographically 2/3 of the Russian Far East population is located in the so-called "Southern zone," the narrow belt along the China border in Primorye, Khabarovsk and Amur.

Nationalities. The Russian Far East population is dominated by Russians and other Slavs. Yakuts are the only sizable native minority in the Russian Far East. Other native peoples constitute minorities even in national republics named after them: Koriakia (still part of Kamchatka), and Chukotka, formerly part of Magadan.

So far the Russian Far East has managed to avoid major conflicts between ethnic groups.

Workforce

The Russian Far East is unique in many ways. The Russian Far East has the highest share of population of working age (61%) and the lowest share of old people (11%) among all of Russia's regions. Within the Russian Far East, almost 70% of Magadan and Kamchatka inhabitants are of working age.

The share of male and female labor is more equally balanced than in the rest of Russia where females workers are in the majority.

Table 2

Ethnic Structure of the Russian Far East Population in 1992 (%)

Russians	80
Ukranians	8
Belorussians	1.5
Yakuts	3.5
Other Native Peoples	1
Tatars	1
Other	5

Share of Yakuts in the population of Yakutlla Republic went down from 43% (1970) to 33% currently.

More than 90% of the Russian Far East's Korean population live on Sakhalin, where they make up 5% of the population. The Russian Far East, with a Jewish population of approximately 15,000, has a Jewish Autonomous Republic, formerly part of the Khabarovsk krai, now practically independent.

The Russian Far East was always a labor-deficit region where 10% of total demand for labor usually went unsatisfied. As a result, increases in unemployment are not expected to be a major threat to social stability.

In certains areas of the Russian Far East, labor is as scarce as ever. South Yakutiia, for example, experiences an acute short-age of blue collar workers. Neryungri enterprises have had to invite guest workers from Mongolia and China to com-pensate for a labor shortage. The reason: a rather small wage differential set against a rather large real difference in living conditions between the Western regions of Russia and the Russian Far East.

R & D Potential. There are 102 former state-supported re-search centers in the Russian Far East, 2/3 of them located in Vladivostok and Khabarovsk. Research institutes of the Russian Academy of Sciences are many in the Russian Far East but are losing financial resources and employees. In 1992, the number of academic researchers decreased by 13% as central funding of research has declined.

Diagram 2

Russian Far East Population Dynamics   *In thousands*

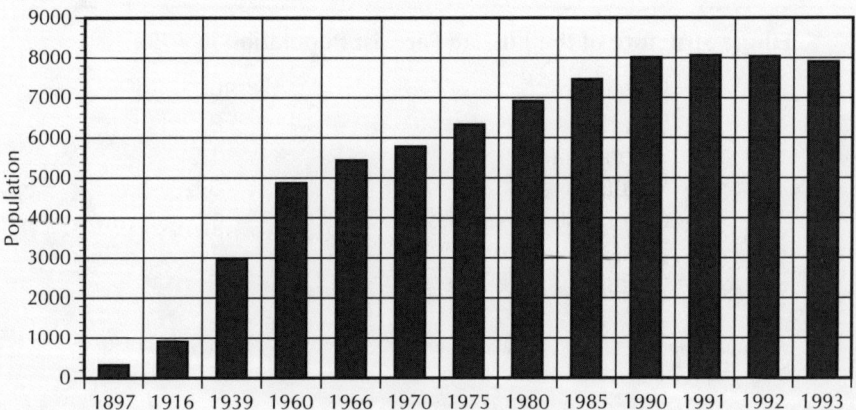

The population of the Russian Far East grew almost 8 times during the Soviet period, while the total USSR population increased by only 60%.

Table 3

Russian Far East Population Change: Natural Growth and Migration (1991 as compared to 1990)

	Natural Growth	Migration	Net Change
Yakutiia (Sakha)	12,300	-17,600	-5,600
Primorye	7,700	2,000	9,700
Khabarovsk	7,800	500	8,300
Amur	5,600	-4,100	1,500
Kamchatka	2,500	0	2,500
Magadan	3,600	-24,400	-20,800
Sakhalin	2,600	-700	1,900
Russian Far East	42,100	-44,300	-2,500

Diagram 3

Urban Population as a Percentage of Total

as of January 1, 1993

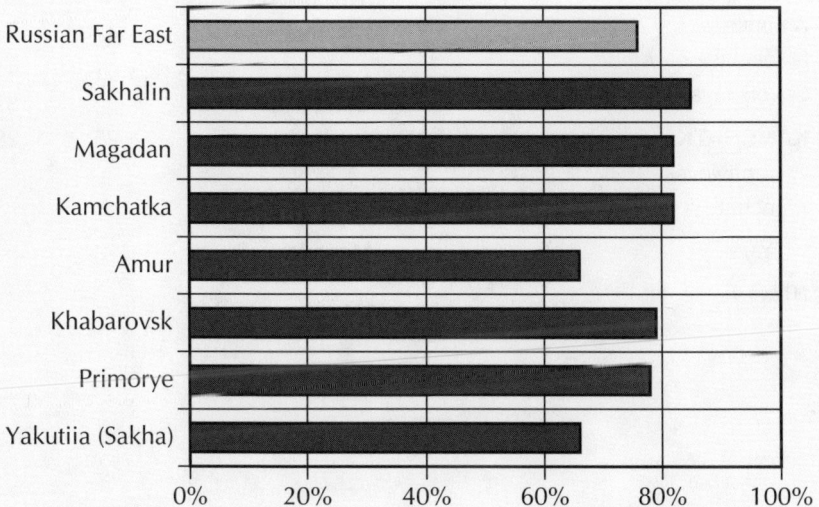

Table 4

Russian Far East Cities and Towns with Populations of more than 25,000 (at the beginning of the year)
in Thousands

	1976	1992		1976	1992
PRIMORYE			**AMUR**		
Vladivostok	526	648	Blagoveschensk	171	214
Nakhodka	127	166	Svobodnyi	70	81
Ussuriisk	145	161	Belogorsk	64	75
Bolshoi Kamen	34	82	Tynda	19	63
Arsenev	58	72	Zeya	27	32*
Artyom	69	70	Shimanovsk	22	27*
Spassk-Dalnyi	52	61	Raichikhinsk	28	27*
Dalnegorsk	41	50	**YAKUTIIA-SAKHA**		
Partizansk	49	50*	Yakutsk	143	198
Lesozavodsk	39	45*	Neryngri	5	76
Dalnerechensk	33	34*	Mirnyi	29	40*
KHABAROVSK			Lensk	22	31*
Khabarovsk	513	615	Aldan	22	27*
Komsomolsk-on-Amur	246	319	**SAKHALIN**		
Birobidzhan	65	87	Yuzhno-Sakhalinsk	131	165
Amursk	35	60	Kholmsk	47	51
Nikolaevsk-on-Amur	34	37*	Korsakov	41	45*
Sovetskaya Gavan	32	35*	Okha	32	37*
KAMCHATKA			Poronaisk	25	26*
Petropavlovsk-Kamchatskii	202	273	**MAGADAN**		
Elizovo	33	49*	Magadan	112	152

*These data are for 1991.

Table 5

Education: College and Other Graduates* per 1000 Employees

	1 College Graduates	2 Graduates from Vocational & Special Schools*	Total (1 + 2)
Yakutiia (Sakha)	134	700	834
Primorye	161	586	747
Khabarovsk	159	569	728
Amur	143	572	715
Kamchatka	179	675	854
Magadan	154	687	841
Sakhalin	136	652	788
RFE	153	616	769
RUSSIA	146	591	737

NOTE: * Including College Graduates with incomplete programs.

The educational level in the Russian Far East, and in Russia in general, is high. However, the Russian Far East average might be inflated by high levels in territories that are national autonomies or those that have (for the purpose of statistical estimation) such enclaves: Yakutiia Republic, Magadan (with Chukotka) and Kamchatka (with Koriakiia). Soviet national policy heavily relied on affirmative action, creating vast numbers of "minority" specialists. The more modest levels of Primorye and Khabarovsk, where the majority of educational and research potential is located, would be a more reliable indicator.

Diagram 4

Number of divorces per every 10 marriages in the Russian Far East

| | 1975 | | 1992 |

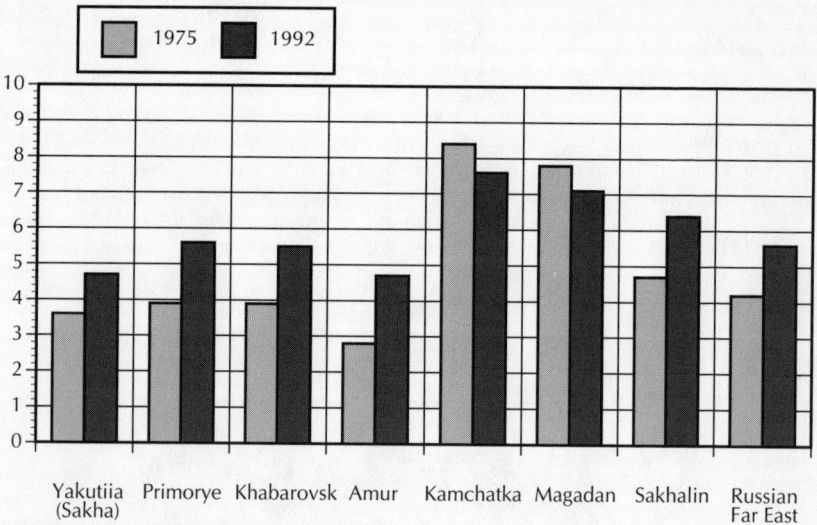

Other Publications from *Russian Far East Update:*

The Fundamentals of a Business Plan: *In English and Russian on facing pages.* This manual describes in simple yet precise terms what a business plan should contain. The author describes a business plan in terms of six separate sections — business mission, ownership, governance and management, management and sales, operations, and financial projections — and outlines the questions each section should answer.

24 pages.   *$37.50 plus shipping & handling.*

Major Ports of the Russian Far East: This manual focuses on the region's nine principal commercial trade ports. For each of the ports we feature a map, contact information, and details of port specialization, infrastructure and trends.

12 pages.   *$49.00 plus shipping & handling.*

For Order Information See Order Forms In Back of This Book

CHAPTER 8: HEALTH AND HOUSING

Introduction.

Infant mortality rates in the Russian Far East are higher than the Russian average. Adult mortality (while somewhat lower than the Russian average, perhaps due to the more youthful population in general) is increasing.

The general crisis in health care certainly has not escaped the Russian Far East. Health services to a great extent have been a responsibility of the enterprise where workers are

Diagram 1

Russian Far East Adult Mortality Rates

(deaths per 1,000)

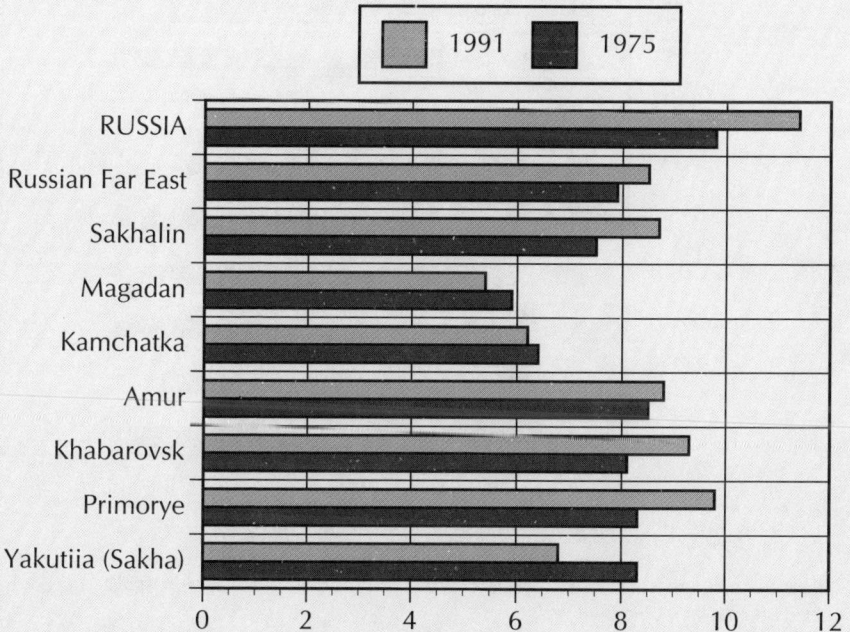

employed. When the enterprise faces collapse, so does the
workers' network of social and health services. Lack of equipment in clinics and hospitals and medicine characterize
health service in the Russian Far East.

Diagram 2

Russian Far East Infant Mortality Rates

(deaths of infants who die before reaching 1 year of age per 1,000 live births)

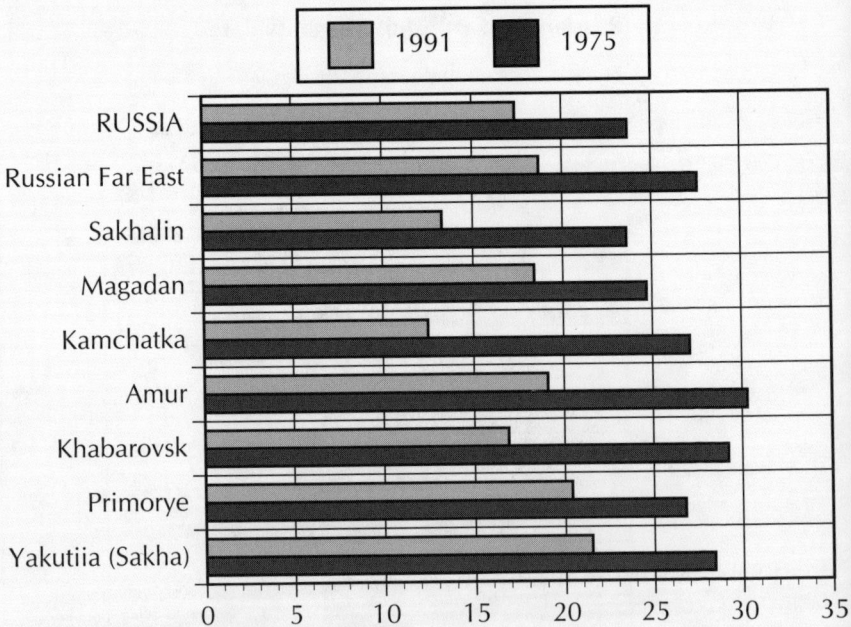

| | 1991 | | 1975 |

RUSSIA
Russian Far East
Sakhalin
Magadan
Kamchatka
Amur
Khabarovsk
Primorye
Yakutiia (Sakha)

0   5   10   15   20   25   30   35

Infant mortality rate in the RFE was 7% higher than the Russian average in 1991. It was 16%
higher than the Russian average in 1975. In the US the infant mortality rate is below 10 per
thousand. Although the chart shows lower rates in 1991 than in 1975, 1992 statistics show an
increase in the infant mortality rate.

Table 1

Russian Far East Health System in 1991

	Doctors *(in thousands)*	Doctors per 10,000 of population	Hospitals[†]	# Beds per 10,000 of population
Yakutiia (Sakha)	4.8	43.1	303	160
Primorye	11.9	51.4	184	139
Khabarovsk	10	54.3	188	147
Amur	5.1	47.9	138	140
Kamchatka	2.6	53.8	69	154
Magadan	2.5	48.4	94	161
Sakhalin	3.1	43.2	82	161
Russian Far East	40	49.7	1,058	148
RUSSIA	650	43.8	12,800	135

[†] In 1990.

Table 2

Living Space in the Russian Far East   *in m² per person*

Yakutiia (Sakha)	13.5
Primorye	14.6
Khabarovsk	15.3
Amur	13.2
Kamchatka	12.4
Magadan	14.8
Sakhalin	15.3
Russian Far East	14.4
Russia	15.7

Housing (mostly apartments) in the Russian Far East is insufficient even by modest Russian standards and of poor quality. Until very recently 95% of all housing construction relied on state investments. New housing construction has fallen with cuts in state capital outlays.

Table 3

Housing Amenities in Russian Far East Cities (1991)

(% of total apartments equipped with amenities)

	Running Water	Hot Water	Sewage Collection	Central Heating	Bathtubs	Natural Gas
Vladivostok	93	89	92	93	86	2
Khabarovsk	87	84	85	92	83	78
Petropavlovsk-Kamchatskii	98	56	95	94	90	0
Blagoveshchensk	83	79	83	83	79	53
Yakutsk	73	63	66	85	61	53
Yuzhno-Sakhalinsk	91	89	90	99	87	0
Magadan	91	89	90	99	87	0
Russian Far East (all urban cities)	89	70	76	91	82	29

Huge and inefficiently run central-heating systems are the trademarks of Russian cities. Lack of hot water in winter (and cold water in the summer, because the system is turned off for "repairs") is a frequent occurence in the Russian Far East. Notice that Yuzhno-Sakhalinsk, a capital of the major oil & gas province in the Russian Far East, does not use gas at all, while Khabarovsk utilizes it to the fullest extent among the Russian Far East territories. Presently Sakhalin is less and less willing to ship its natural gas to the mainland, which may cause problems for Khabarovsk households.

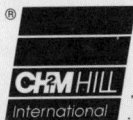

Table 4

Crime and Punishment in the Russian Far East (1993)

	Crimes registered per 1,000 population	Percentage of Cases solved
Yakutiia	15.06	0.57
Primorye	30.39	0.42
Khabarovsk	26.18	0.51
Amur	17.73	0.54
Kamchatka	19.09	0.47
Magadan	18.80	0.51
Sakhalin	29.03	0.35
RUSSIA	16.75	0.49

Cities in Primorye, Sakhalin and Khabarovsk—large and open to the "outside world"—have the most crime. Crime is usually higher in port cities. It also seems that the police are least efficient (in terms of share of cases solved) in the areas that are hit hardest.

CHAPTER 9: INDUSTRY

OVERVIEW

The Russian Far East produces just 5% of Russia's total industrial output. However, in a number of areas, it contributes much more significantly to the national economy. The region provides, for example, almost 60% of Russia's catch of fish and sea products. The Russian Far East is second only to West Siberia in mining (producing 17% of Russia's national output). Also, the region has a near-monopoly in some items such as tin, gold, diamonds, tungsten, antimony.

In some sectors, however, the situation is the reverse. For example, the Russian Far East's iron & steel industry, its chemical sector, and its textile industry produce well below Russia's national average. Machine building, with a heavy portion in the defense sector, needs much restructuring.

Territorial Structure. Industrial production is concentrated in the South of the Russian Far East. Khabarovsk and Primorye are relatively diversified and self-sufficient. The northern areas are mostly tundra and taiga, with isolated pockets of industrial activity. Sakhalin, and especially Kamchatka, are heavily dependent on fishing and fish processing.

Industry Structure. Industrial production in the Russian Far East territories is dominated by fishing, mining (nonferrous metals) and logging and timber processing.

Table 1

Russian Far East's Contribution to Russia's Industrial Output (%)

Mining	16.4
Manufacturing	3.7
Nonferrous metals	16.1
Timber Industry	8.0
Fishing Industry	58.0

Data are for 1991.

Because of the relatively low level of diversification of local industry, some basic industrial goods have to be imported, mainly from other Russian regions. For example, every Russian Far East Territory (except Khabarovsk) imports 100% of its rolled stock and oil products needs.

Industrial Crises. For decades the Russian Far East was growing faster than the rest of Russia. With the dissolution of the USSR economy and the continuing economic crisis since 1991, the Russian Far East has been one of the regions

Diagram 1

**Russian Far East Total Industrial Output
by Territory**

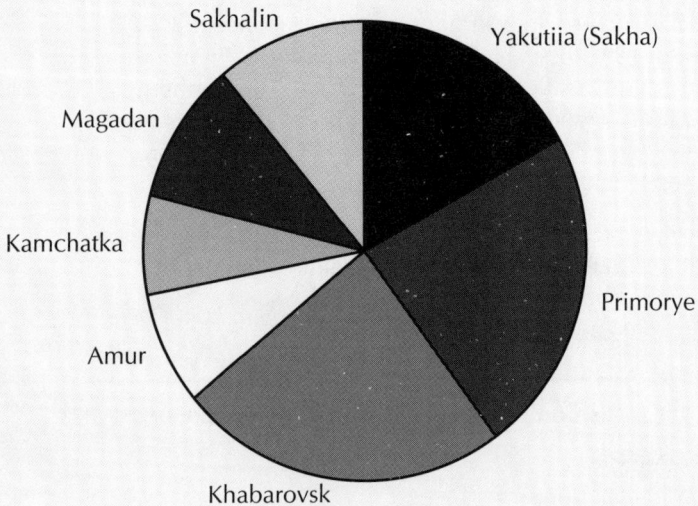

Data are for 1991.

hit the worst. In the days of the USSR, Moscow invested heavily to develop Russian Far East industries that served "all-union" needs. Now both money (and, in some cases, markets) are gone and the region has had to adjust its economy.

The Russian Far East's industrial slump is accompanied by financial difficulties of many enterprises in many sectors of the local economy, although bankruptcies are still rare.

Diagram 2

Decrease in Industrial Output Since 1991

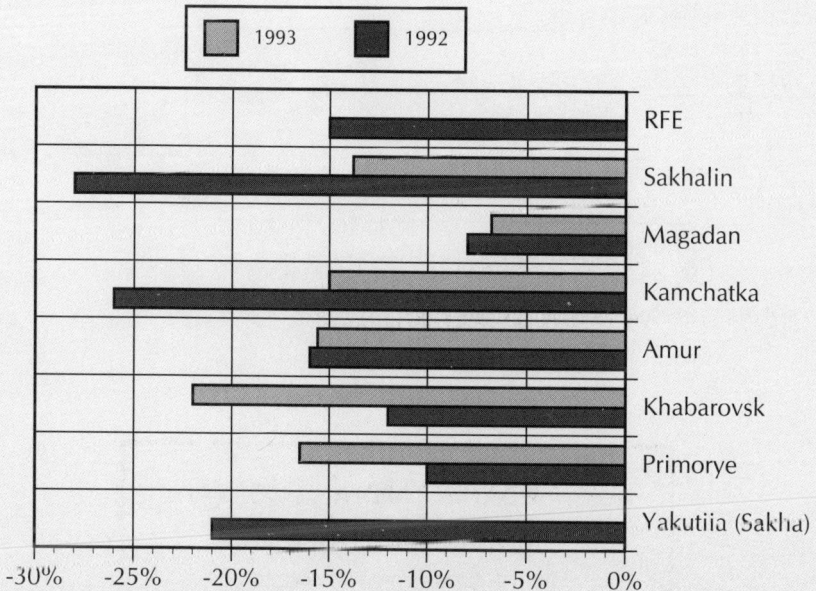

Legend: 1993, 1992

Categories: RFE, Sakhalin, Magadan, Kamchatka, Amur, Khabarovsk, Primorye, Yakutiia (Sakha)

Axis: -30%, -25%, -20%, -15%, -10%, -5%, 0%

Table 2

Structure of Industrial Production by Territory   *in percentage*

	RFE	Yakutiia	Primorye	Khabarovsk	Amur	Kamchatka	Magadan	Sakhalin
TOTAL	100	100	100	100	100	100	100	100
Electric Energy	3	3	2	3	6	5	6	2
Fuel Industry	4	6	1	7	3	0	1	5
Iron & Steel Industry	1	0	0	4	0	0	0	0
Nonferrous Metals	19	63	4	5	13	1	59	0
Chemical & Petrochemical	2	0	3	4	0	0	0	0
Machine Building	15	2	21	29	14	8	6	5
Timber, Pulp & Paper	9	4	6	12	10	3	2	29
Food Industry*	34	12	48	21	39	74	16	50
Light Industry	4	1	5	7	5	2	3	2
Building Materials	7	7	8	6	8	6	5	5
Other	2	9	14	15	14	9	9	9

* Food industry includes fish and fish processing.

Data are for 1991.

Diagram 3

Share of Non-Profitable Enterprises in the Russian Far East Economy in 1992 (% of total): by Territory

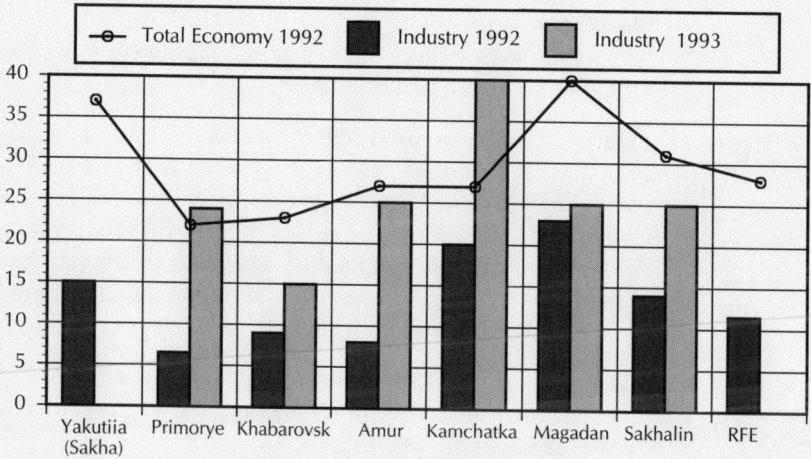

Legend: Total Economy 1992 · Industry 1992 · Industry 1993

X-axis: Yakutiia (Sakha), Primorye, Khabarovsk, Amur, Kamchatka, Magadan, Sakhalin, RFE

Diagram 4

Overdue Loans as a Percentage of Total Credits Extended to the Russian Far East Economy (beginning of the year)

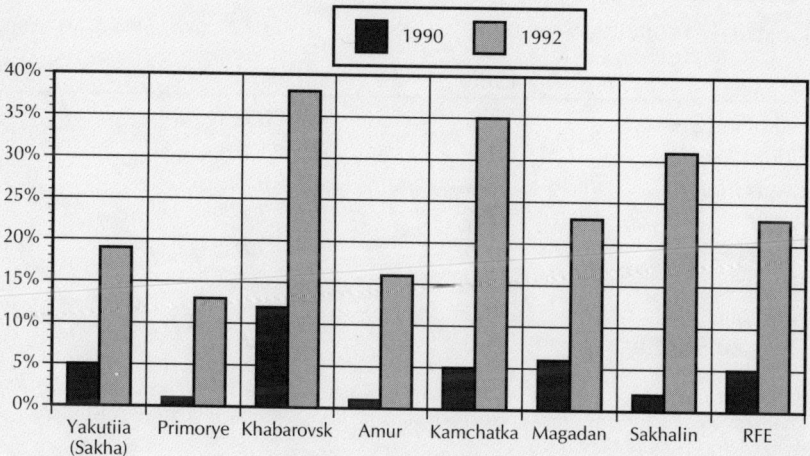

Legend: 1990 · 1992

X-axis: Yakutiia (Sakha), Primorye, Khabarovsk, Amur, Kamchatka, Magadan, Sakhalin, RFE

EXTRACTIVE INDUSTRIES

Energy (including Oil & Gas)

The Energy Sector of the Russian Far East comprises coal, oil & gas recovery, oil processing, production of electric and heat energy (including nuclear generation). With less than 5% of the total employment, this sector controls 1/3 of the region's industrial assets.

Electricity & heat production. Energy production in the Russian Far East relies heavily on shipments of coal into the southern regions. The coal is usually of low quality and shipments are often irregular. In general, reserves of electricity-generating capacities, as well as of fuel, are low. The Russian Far East power grid is insufficiently developed, some areas are chronically deficit.

Out of 244 major power plants (i.e., those that are linked to the national grid system), 5 account for almost 40% of installed capacity.

Table 3

Electricity Production   *in billion Kilowatt-hours*

	1985	1990	1992
Yakutiia (Sakha)	5.5	8.5	7.4
Primorye	11.6	11.8	11.0
Khabarovsk	5.4	9.7	9.3
Amur	7.1	7.8	6.9
Kamchatka	1.5	1.9	1.8
Magadan	3.9	4.4	3.8
Sakhalin	3.0	3.4	2.8
Russian Far East	38.0	47.5	43.0

In the last decade, production of electricity was increasing in Yakutiia and in Khabarovsk. Khabarovsk, a major consumer of electricity and far from self sufficient, draws electricity from its neighbors (Amur oblast, etc.).

Diagram 5

Electricity Production by Type of Power Plant

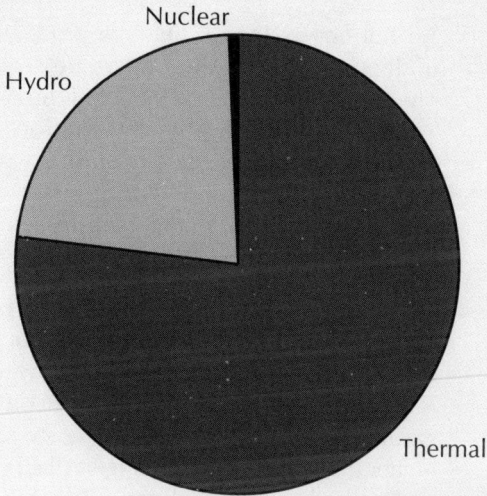

The only nuclear power plant (PP) in the RFE is located at Bilibino (Chukotka) with installed capacity of 48 MW, supplying heat to a nearby major mining complex. Major hydro PPs are located at Zeya, Kolyma and Viluy rivers and in Southern Primorye.

Table 4

Major Russian Far East Power Plants

	Type	Installed Generating Capacity (MW)	Location
Primorskaia	Thermal	1495	Primorye
Zeya	Hydro	1330	Amur
Kolyma	Hydro	720	Magadan
Viliui	Hydro	648	Yakutiia
Khabarovsk-3	HEGS*	540	Khabarovsk

NOTE: * HEGS = Heat Electric Generating Station.

Russian Far East Oil & Gas Industry. Many of the Russian Far East regions have, or are thought to have, oil and gas reserves. Production, however, is restricted to two areas: Northern Sakhalin and Central Yakutiia.

All but one of the oil fields in production are located on northern Sakhalin. All of them are small or medium size. The only large operating oil field is Sredne-Botoubinskoe in Yakutiia with more than 30 million tons of confirmed reserves. In recent years a number of plans to develop substantial offshore oil and gas reserves have been proposed, mainly off-shore Sakhalin, and to some extent, off-shore Magadan.

Russian Far East oil is usually sweet, i.e., with low sulfur content (below 0.5%) and only 20% of the output is heavy oil. Usually, the ash content is also low (less than 0.5%). Oil is recovered mainly by pumps and compressors (including gaslifting). Russian Far East oil costs are 5 times or more higher than the Russian average. All currently producing oil wells are located onshore. Oil production is steadily declining from record levels reached in the mid-80's (2.5-2.6 million tons); many of the Sakhalin fields are exhausted.

The only Russian Far East oil pipeline connects Sakhalin with Komsomolsk-on-Amur's oil refinery plant. In the early 1990's, approx. 1.5 million tons were carried annually.

Tables 5 & 6

Oil production (including gas condensate)   *1000 tons*

	1985	1990	1992
Sakhalin	2 597	1850	1670
Yakutiia (Sakha)	0	41	130
Russian Far East	2 597	1891	1800

Natural Gas production   *million cubic meters*

	1985	1990	1992
Sakhalin	809	1832	1780
Yakutiia (Sakha)	1017	1402	1540
Russian Far East	1826	3234	3320

The natural gas industry is doing better. Production is almost equally divided between 25 small and medium Sakhalin onshore wells (with 10 billion m³) and three relatively large Yakutian gas fields (with 30 billion m³).

Two gas pipe lines are in operation: one joins Yakutsk with the Viliui basin fields, another goes from Sakhalin to Komsomolsk-on-Amur. The latter pipeline, designed to carry 4.5 billion m³, only utilizes 1/4 of its capacity.

Like oil, Russian Far East gas is far more expensive (3-5 times) to recover than Russian natural gas on the average. Oil and gas production require heavy budget subsidies.

Oil-processing. Russian Far East has only 2 oil-refining plants, both in Khabarovsk krai: in Khabarovsk city (4.5 million tons/year) and in Komsomolsk-on-Amur (5.6 million tons/year). These plants cover only 40% of regional demand, so that the Russian Far East has to import approximately 12 million tons of oil products annually. Crude oil comes from Sakhalin (15%) through a pipeline to Komsomolsk plant and from Western Siberia (85%) by rail.

Coal Industry. Coal is the major source of fuel for energy production in every Russian Far East territory except Kamchatka. The bulk of the Russian Far East's coal deposits are found in Primorye, Yakutiia and Amur.

Table 7

Production of Coal   *million tons*

	1985	1990	1992
Yakutiia (Sakha)	14.2	17.0	12.7
Primorye	18.3	16.0	13.0
Khabarovsk	1.9	2.2	1.9
Amur	9.0	6.8	5.5
Kamchatka	0.1	0.1	4.5
Magadan	3.5	3.2	0.1
Sakhalin	5.0	5.0	3.4
Russian Far East	51.7	49.9	40.7

A few enterprises account for most of coal mining in the Russian Far East: 5 state-supported concerns, 2-3 mines (local property) and 1-2 are semiprivate mines.

There are 35 mines and 15 open cuts in the region. The majority of coal mined comes from open cuts (75%). Almost half of Russian Far East coal is brown. The region produces 6 million tons of coking coal per year.

Huge investments in the coal industry have not prevented a decrease in the capacity due to closing of old mines. Coal mining has fallen from 57.2 million tons in 1988, an all-time high, to 40.6 million tons in 1992. As a result, the Russian Far East had to import about 20% of its total coal consumption from Siberia and Mongolia.

Diagram 6

Relative Cost of Coal Production in Early 1990s

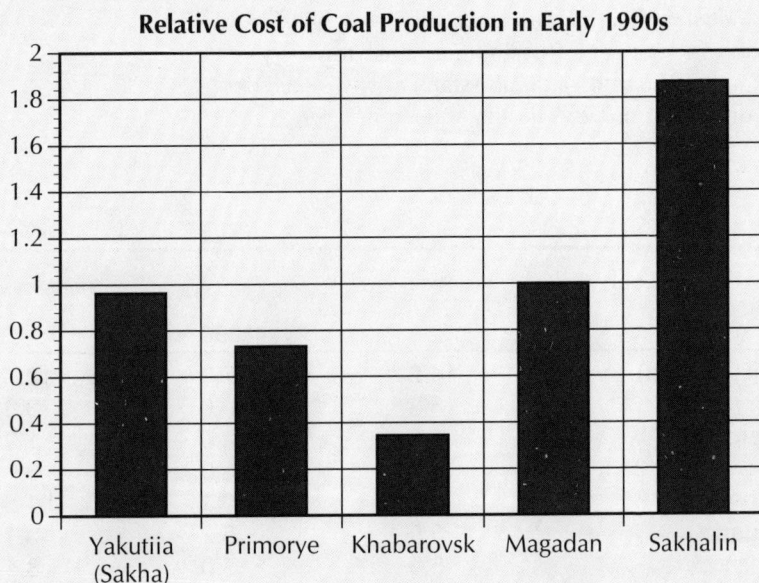

NOTE: Costs of Magadan coal industry are taken for the unit of measurement

Coal mining in the Russian Far East is costly by Russian standards. Even Amur coal, the cheapest to mine is twice as expensive as coal mining in Siberia. As a result the Russian Far East coal mining industry was, and still is, highly subsidized.

Mining Industry

The Russian Far East is one of the key mining regions for Russia.

Diamonds. Diamonds are mined from kimberlite popes and mines. Major producers are "Udachnyii" ore-dressing combine (80% of total output) with 4 processing plants, and "Myrnyii" mine with 2 processing plants. Both entities are parts of state-supported "Almazy Yakutii-Sakha" company. Explored reserves will support production only until the year 2000, additional exploration is necessary.

Table 8

Russia's Mining Industry: Russian Far East Share of Total Output

Item	Share in Russia's Total Output	Estimates* of Annual Russian Far East Output, early 1990's
Diamonds	99.8%	10-30 million carats
Gold		90-100 tons
Silver		300 tons
Platinum		3-4 tons
Tin	95%	20-22 thousand tons
Lead	appr. 50%	26-28 thousand tons
Zinc	appr. 50%	36-38 thousand tons
Tungsten†	48%	
Antimony	100%	23-24 thousand tons

†including Chita.

Gold. Gold production is decreasing, despite the entrance of new commercial entities. State producers are still the most important.

Four major state-supported companies are:

Severovostokzoloto	Magadan and Kamchatka
Yakutzoloto	Yakutiia and northern Khabarovsk krai
Amurzoloto	Amur oblast
Primorzoloto	Primorye, Sakhalin, Khabarovsk

These companies include 16 ore-dressing combines and other entities.

Prospector teams, a second major producer in the industry, work in placers, using bulldozers and other simple machinery. In Khabarovsk krai, prospector teams mine 3/4 of all gold.

Silver. All silver is mined from complex gold, polymetallic and other deposits. Major producers: Magadan (where silver is mined jointly with gold) and Primorye (where silver is mined jointly with tin, lead and zinc).

Reserves are sufficient to increase production 2-3 times by 2000 and support it on that level for 25 years.

Table 9

Gold mining output in the Russian Far East in 1992   in kilograms

Magadan*	43,236	33.3%
Yakutiia (Sakha)	30,515	23.5%
Amur	10,222	7.8%
Khabarovsk	7,514	5.8%
Primorye	244	0.1%
Sakhalin	190	0.1%
Kamchatka	152	0.1%
Russian Far East	**92,075**	**71.0%**
Russia	**129,520**	**100.0%**

NOTE: *Including Chukotka

Platinum. All platinum is mined at the Konder gold-platinum deposit (Khabarovsk's Aiano-Maiskii district, 3 grams of metal per ton of ores) by "Amur" prospector teams. Annual output was 3.5 tons in 1993. Confirmed reserves can support production for 20 years.

Lead & Zinc. The Russian Far East (24 explored deposits) produces about one half of Russia's lead & zinc output. More than 90% is provided by state-supported Production Association "Dalpolimetall." The latter produces some refined lead at its processing plant in Primorye. Reserves can support production for almost 50 years.

Tin. The Russian Far East (35 deposits in production) accounts for 95% of Russia's tin output. Major producers are Yakutiia (35% of regional output), Khabarovsk (27% of regional output), Primorye (22% of regional output) and Magadan & Chukotka (16% of regional output). Lode deposits account for 80% of the output.

Khabarovsk krai (Khingan ore-dressing combine) has the lowest production costs in Russia, while Magadan-mined tin ore is the most expensive. Reserves are quite sufficient for current production levels.

Tungsten. Russian Far East (55 explored deposits) and Transbaikalia mine almost half of Russian tungsten ores. Primorye accounts for 28% of Russia's output now, while Chita and Magadan produce 10% each. Khabarovsk and Yakutiia also participate in production.

Antimony. All of Russian mining of antimony is concentrated in 2 Yakutian deposits. All ore-processing is done outside of the region.

Timber, Pulp & Paper Industry

The Timber, Pulp and Paper Industry combines logging, wood-processing, production of pulp & paper, and accounts for 10-15% of the Russian Far East industrial employment and output.

Table 10

Output of Forest Products: by Territory

1000 cubic meters

Industrial Roundwood	1985	1991
Yakutiia (Sakha)	3,882	2821
Primorye	6,136	3954
Khabarovsk	13,823	10369
Amur	5905	4,928
Kamchatka	949	690
Magadan	369	195
Sakhalin	3388	2,711
Russian Far East	34452	25,668

Lumber	1985	1991 *1000 cubic meters*
Yakutiia (Sakha)	810	613
Primorye	1495	842
Khabarovsk	2075	1683
Amur	756	727
Kamchatka	270	170
Magadan	188	102
Sakhalin	585	411
Russian Far East	6179	4548

Sawn Timber	1985	1991 *1000 cubic meters*
Yakutiia (Sakha)	810	613
Primorye	1495	842
Khabarovsk	2075	1683
Amur	756	727
Kamchatka	270	170
Magadan	188	102
Sakhalin	585	411
Russian Far East	6179	4548

Pulp	1985	1991 *1000 tons*
Khabarovsk	250	240
Sakhalin	323	267
Russian Far East	573	507

Paper	1985	1991 *1000 tons*
Sakhalin	216	200
Khabarovsk	9	5
Amur	3.5	3
Russian Far East	228.5	208

Because of many irrationalities in the logging process, the share of mature trees, as well as density of stands and stock, is decreasing. Because artificial regeneration is not pursued actively, the share of less valuable hardwood species is increasing. Forest fires are now the major problem in stock preservation. In the 1980's, fires damaged more than 1 million acres of forests annually. This was almost equal to the area harvested by the industry. However, despite primitive reforestation and devastating forest fires, total forested area in the Russian Far East has been *on the rise* since the 1970's.

Total annual allowable cut (AAC)–which determines the upper level of logging–in the Russian Far East is set at 100-110 ml m^3 (85% in softwood species). Between 1/3-1/2 of the quota is used, depending on the specific area. The huge surplus, however, is deceiving since the AAC is not an economic measure: it tells nothing about costs in general, nor about accessibility of timber in particular. Another fact here is that 50% of the total AAC is in larch, a species that finds limited demand on the world markets.

Logging, not processing, is the major, and sometimes the only activity for many Russian Far East territories. Harvesting is mechanized, major pieces of equipment are Russian-made motor-saws, skidders, fellers and buncher-fellers. A long history of timber exports to Japan has helped the Russian Far East to import large quantities of Japanese trucks and some stationary processing equipment. Recently Russian Far East loggers have started to buy foreign-built harvesters and forwarders. Government regulations aimed at containing

Table 11

Processed Wood Products in the Russian Far East

	Plywood 1000 m³		Fiberboards million conv. m³		Chipboards 1000 conv. m³	
	1985	**1991**	**1985**	**1991**	**1985**	**1991**
Primorye	23.5	7	1.5	1	74.5	94
Khabarovsk	11	7.5	21	19	40.5	92
Amur	1	.05	0	0	0	0
Russian Far East	35.5	15	22.5	20	115	186

ecological damage (limits on soil pressure, for example) have been strengthened and are even enforced — to some degree. This creates another stimulus to look for foreign-built machinery.

Timber processing occurs mainly in Khabarovsk and Primorye: industrial chip production, fibre and particle board.

In all the Russian Far East, output is decreasing. Private enterprises are relatively few in this sector because of the large initial value of investments required and the unresolved question of timber land ownership.

Sakhalin and Khabarovsk are the major centers of pulp & paper production in the region. All seven Sakhalin Japanese-built (1914-1935) plants are outdated. Several Japanese companies are negotiating modernization and expansion. The relatively modern largest single plant producing paper (in Amursk, Khabarovsk krai) still cannot assure stable production and suffers from electricity brownouts.

Some of the other economic uses of Russian Far East forests are worth mentioning too: furs, hunting, tourism.

Table 12

Fish & Other Products of the Sea: Catch   *million tons*

	1985	1990	1991	1992
Yakutiia (Sakha)	9	10	7	N. A.
Primorye	1573	1832	1586	1350
Khabarovsk	317	370	301	157
Amur*	0	0	0	0
Kamchatka	1242	1348	1211	879
Magadan	93	140	101	126
Sakhalin	959	928	856	628
RFE	4193	4628	4062	3140

*Amur does not have access to saltwater fishing.

Fishing and fish processing

Fishing and fish processing is a very important sector of Russian Far East's extractive industry. The industry, in 1992, operated 1,400 vessels, (almost 900 of them large and medium size), and employed 156,000 workers. This sector includes harvesting, processing, ship repairing, production of packaging materials, etc.

Total allowable harvest for the Russian Far East is estimated, on the average, in excess of 5 million tons. This is much higher than the actual (reported) harvesting. Still, many Russian Far East fishing enterprises complain of insufficient resources and annual distribution of quotas among Russian Far East territories is becoming more complicated every year.

Diagram 7

Output and Employment in Fish & Fish Processing in the Russian Far East

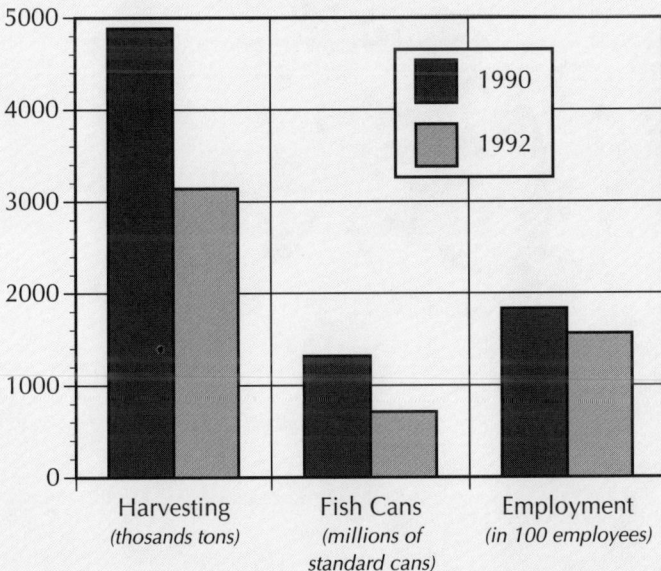

Fishing is limited to a handful of species: Alaskan pollack, Far Eastern pilchard (*ivasi*), salmon. Harvesting of these species has been substantially affected by intensive foreign fishing in the central (international) area of Okhotsk Sea according to Russian fishery experts. Underutilized species include anchovy (potentially 100 thousand tons of annual harvesting), cod, halibut, and saury—in some areas 100-140 thousand tons together. Fish farming, except for salmon, is still undeveloped.

The structure of the fishing industry consists of state-supported enterprises, fishing collective farms, commercial enterprises, and joint ventures.

Diagram 8

Russian Far East Fish & Marine Harvesting

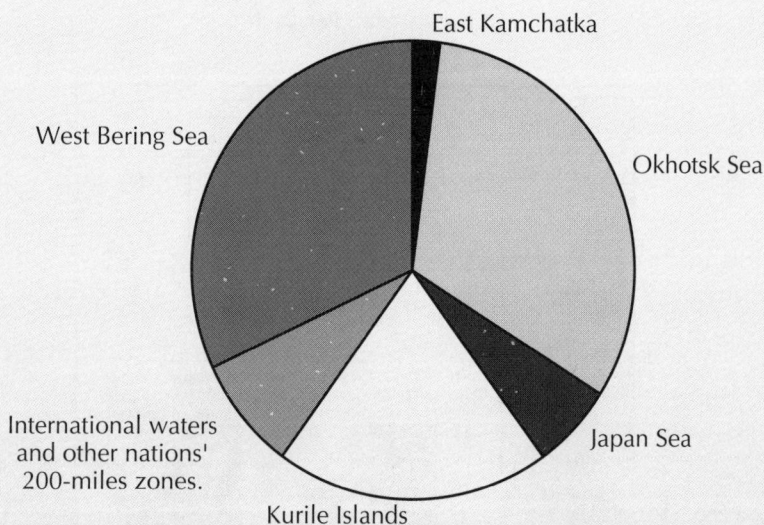

East Kamchatka

West Bering Sea

Okhotsk Sea

International waters and other nations' 200-miles zones.

Japan Sea

Kurile Islands

NOTE: Every area is within Russia's exclusive 200-mile economic zone, if not specified otherwise. More than 90% of all Russian Far East fish is harvested within Russian Far East 200-mile economic zone.

Until recently the Russian Far East fishing industry was almost completely controlled by the giant regional state association "Dalryba" which supervised up to 75% of all fishing and fish processing. By the end of 1992, under privatization, all state concerns were transformed into closed joint stock companies.

The industry is becoming more competitive. "Dalryba," now a "voluntary" association, still exists, but many of its former members, mainly located outside of Primorye, have decided to try business on their own.

Collective farms, united in territorial associations, are a vital part of this industry. At the end of 1992, this group of about 50 enterprises owned 395 small- and medium-size harvesting vessels. Their own processing base is undeveloped. Collective farms formed a number of joint ventures with foreign partners.

Joint ventures in the industry, according to official statistics, accounted for just 1% of all Russian Far East fish caught, but a much larger percentage of exports. There were more than 50 fishing & processing joint ventures in the Russian Far East at the end of 1992, 20 of them with Japanese partners.

The industry's fish processing base is antiquated: the majority of its 32 shore-based processing plants were built in 1930's and 40's.

Ship repair is doing no better: regional centers can meet less than half of demand for these services, requiring about 10 times longer than foreign firms to perform comparable operations. As a result Russian vessels are often sent to neighboring countries for repair. The greater part of the Russian Far East fleet (95% of factory vessels, for example) is physically obsolete. Replacing the fleet is a new priority of the industry.

MANUFACTURING & PROCESSING

The Iron & Steel Industry of the Russian Far East is represented by just one plant, "Amurstal" (Komsomolsk-on-Amur). It produces 97% of all steel and 100% of rolled products of the region. Pig iron and iron scrap are imported from Western Siberia. "Amurstal" manufactures only certain products and as a result the region has to import some items.

Machine building is divided between civilian and defense enterprises. Eighty-six civilian enterprises throughout the Russian Far East specialize in a limited assortment of items: equipment for energy plants, mining, and agriculture. Khabarovsk and Primorye account for 4/5 of the output of this sector. Large civilian complexes in Khabarovsk krai produce travelling electric cranes, gas turbines, power transformers, grain and feeder harvesters, lathes, car batteries, diesel engines, etc. Primorye enterprises specialize in household appliances, almost all of them produced at defense sector plants.

Table 13

Steel Output in the Russian Far East   *in thousand tons*

	1985	1990	1991
Steel production			
Khabarovsk	1044	1383	1168
Magadan	12	10	10
Primorye	6	7	7
Amur	9	6	5
Yakutiia (Sakha)	1	1	1
Sakhalin	1	1	1
Russian Far East	1073	1408	1192
Rolled Steel production			
Khabarovsk	986	1211	1020
Russian Far East	986	1211	1020

The defense sector, with 32 major enterprises, is one of the most important industrial sectors in the Russian Far East. Production is diversified, but the plants specialize primarily in shipbuilding (including nuclear submarines) and avionics. Defense production is concentrated mainly at Vladivostok, Komsomolsk-on-Amur and Khabarovsk. In some centers, like Arsenev or Bolshoi Kamen (both in Primorye), these enterprises account for 90-98% of total industrial production.

The Chemical Industry is not a major sector of the Russian Far East economy. Still, the region produces most of Russia's borum and borum products and fluorite.

All borum production is concentrated in Dalnegorsk in Primorye deposit where 90% total confirmed Russian borum reserves are concentrated. Fluorite production is also concentrated in Primorye. The Yaroslavskii ore-dressing combine (Khorolskii district in Primorye) produces 92% of the Russian Far East concentrate from a deposit that holds 70% of the Russian Far East total.

The Russian Far East does not produce at all, or produces in small amounts, such items as fertilizers, soda, basic plastics, etc. Khabarovsk and Primorye krais are the only producers of caustic soda (4,700 tons in 1991), synthetic resins (10,000 tons) and sulfuric acid (520,000 tons) in the Russian Far East.

Table 14

Defense Sector as a Percentage of the Russian Far East Industry in 1991

	RFE	Khabarovsk	Primorye
Defense sector share in the Value of Output	9.5%	23%	14%
Defense sector share in the Value of Assets	6%	17%	10%
Defense sector share in Employment	13%	24%	20%

FOOD AND OTHER CONSUMER GOODS

Consumer goods production is one of the least developed sectors of Russian Far East industry. The regional market is supplied from other regions of Russia and, increasingly, from abroad. In addition, production was hit heavily by the current industrial crisis.

In terms of per capita output of consumer goods (including food and excluding alcohol), the Russian Far East is almost 30% below Russia's average. The region would have done far worse if not for processed fish and fish products. In terms of durable consumer goods, local production in certain products is simply nonexistent.

Food Processing Industry

Local production of food items is insufficient and the Russian Far East imports food in substantial quantities.

Diagram 9

Change in Output of Consumer Goods in 1992 (%)

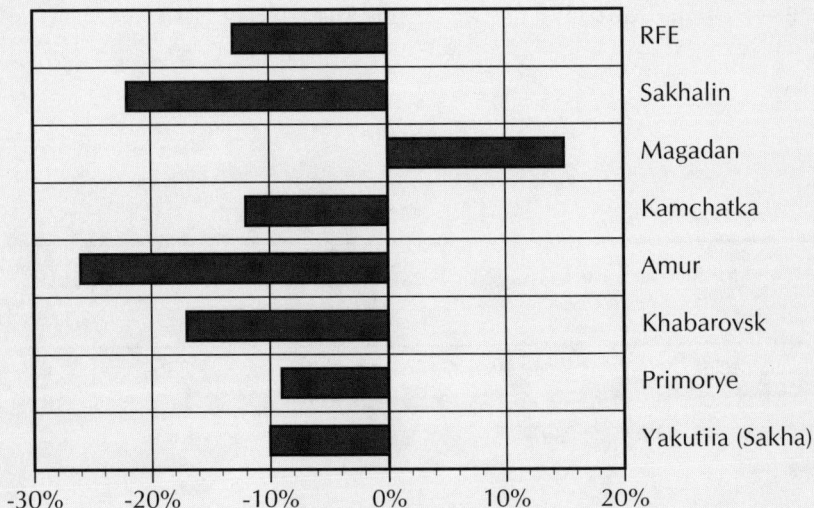

Table 15

Per Capita Consumption of Food Products   *in kg*

	1970	1980	1991
Meat	54	67	66
Milk	343	345	303
Eggs (dozens)	13	276	264
Potatoes	108	95	106
Vegetables	89	109	81
Bread	154	127	115
Fish	25	30	29
Sugar	45	48	43
Vegetable oil	8.5	11	9
Alcoholic beverages*	N. A.	13	5.5†

*in liters of pure alcohol; 1990.

Table 16

Output of Basic Foodstuffs

Meat *thousand tons*	1985	1991	Eggs *millions*	1985*	1991
Yakutiia (Sakha)	23	19	Yakutiia (Sakha)	430	161
Primorye	46	39	Primorye	534	659
Khabarovsk	35	37	Khabarovsk	533	554
Amur	39	44	Amur	262	273
Kamchatka	13	11	Kamchatka	135	133
Magadan	10	13	Magadan	185	165
Sakhalin	16	20	Sakhalin	202	230
Russian Far East	182	183	Russian Far East	1981	2175

* mean production for 1981-1985

Table 16 (continued)

Butter *thousand tons*			**Cheese (fatty)** *tons*		
Yakutiia (Sakha)	4.35	2.7	Yakutiia (Sakha)	75	0
Primorye	0.59	0.7	Primorye	350	400
Khabarovsk	0.01	0	Khabarovsk	0	100
Amur	5.35	7	Amur	171	500
Kamchatka	0.02	0	Kamchatka	0	0
Magadan	0	0	Magadan	0	0
Sakhalin	0.51	0.8	Sakhalin	0	100
Russian Far East	10.83	11.2	Russian Far East	596	1100

Dairy Products *thousand tons*			**Vegetable Oil** *thousand tons*		
Yakutiia (Sakha)	105	124	Primorye	10	10
Primorye	249	237	Khabarovsk	15	16
Khabarovsk	164	182	Amur	2	1
Amur	93	118	Russian Far East	27	27
Kamchatka	63	68			
Magadan	68	70	**Granulated Sugar** *thousand tons*		
Sakhalin	101	106	Primorye	151	134
Russian Far East	843	905			

Flour *thousand tons*			**Bread**		
Yakutiia (Sakha)	0	0	Yakutiia (Sakha)	96	97
Primorye	175	204	Primorye	317	302
Kabarovsk	253	228	Khabarovsk	240	223
Amur	257	259	Amur	151	139
Kamchatka	36	33	Kamchatka	38	41
Magadan	0	0	Magadan	44	40
Sakhalin	56	66	Sakhalin	80	80
Russian Far East	777	790	Russian Far East	966	922

Non-alcoholic Beverages *million dl*			**Canned Food** *million cans*		
Yakutiia (Sakha)	.06	.09	Yakutiia (Sakha)	0	0
Primorye	3.2	4.5	Primorye	657	575
Khabarovsk	2.9	3.4	Khabarovsk	23	29
Amur	1.4	1.6	Amur	12	17
Kamchatka	0.8	0.8	Kamchatka	305	216
Magadan	0.8	0.8	Magadan	16	32
Sakhalin	1.1	1.3	Sakhalin	343	232
Russian Far East	10.8	13	Russian Far East	1356	1101

Light Industry

Light industry in the region was always of secondary importance for Moscow planners. The industry was developed in the Russian Far East mainly to utilize the female workforce and to establish a production base for army needs (uniforms, etc.). Production is based on materials brought from other Russian regions or imported.

The deterioration of economic links among the former Soviet Republics has caused a severe economic slump in this sector. In 1992 production fell by 35-40% and 1993 was not much better. As a result this sector now fails to cover local demand for almost any type of basic item.

Apparel manufacturing is the major sector of the Russian Far East light industry. Almost all of its 250 or so enterprises use imported raw materials (from other parts of Russia and abroad). Almost all of the enterprises in this sector are located

Diagram 10

Relative Shares of Imported and Domestic Consumer Goods

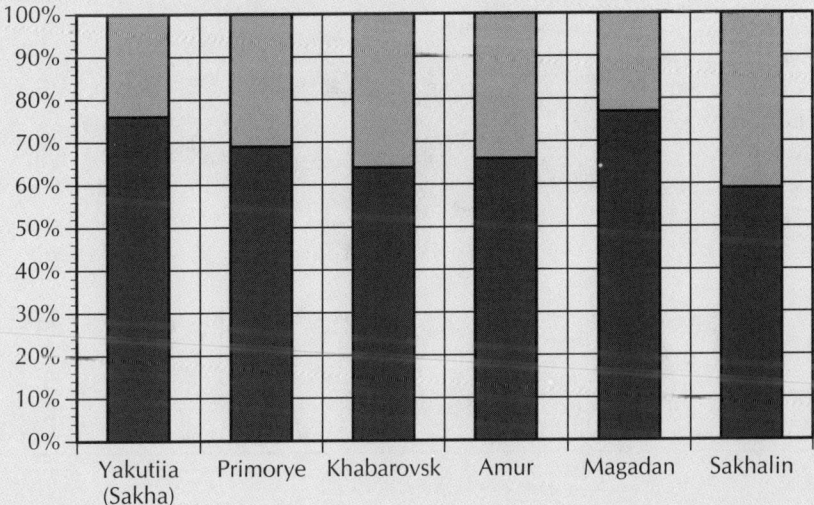

Data are for 1991.
Share of foreign imports varies between 10% and 20% of the total Russian Far East consumer goods.

in the South of the region. Major firms (all of them former state companies) are "Vostok" with 2 major plants–in Khabarovsk and Spassk (Primorye), "Komsomolka (Komsomolsk-on-Amur) and "Zarya" (Vladivostok).

The textile industry in the Russian Far East cover 10-15% of local demand for knitted under- and outerwear. Production is concentrated in Khabarovsk (3 plants) and Primorye (1 plant).

Russian Law: Does it Matter in the Wild East?

Kevin Block

Is the Russian Far East an unruly, lawless place, where lawyers aren't the ones either to structure deals, conduct negotiations or settle disputes? Some might accept the rough 'n' tumble images of the lawless society, picturing the gun-bearing mafia in charge. The notion of the "Wild East" is both accurate and misleading. Yes, by Western standards, the Russian Far East, as Russia in general, is fundamentally lawless, but that does not mean it is prudent to ignore the law.

Many Laws, No Rule of Law

What is the role of Russian law, then, in doing business in the Russian Far East? Some investors, especially big corporations, bring with them the notion that the law is of primary importance: for example, when tax considerations "drive" a transaction by defining its structure, or when corporate and contract law fix the parties' relationship, providing it with stability. In this view, it is the law, most of all, which provides the context or framework for the deal, a set of rules or boundaries which all parties acknowledge and within which they try to work together.

Many laws, no rule of law: investors are doing themselves a disservice if they do not come to grips with this paradox.

Other investors come to do business with the notion that "lawless" means literally that there is no law, or that they can ignore Russian law without suffering negative consequences. They are usually disdainful and ignorant of Russian law and place primary stress on the need to "wire" a deal politically or to "grease the skids" financially.

Both of these approaches miss the meaning of Russian law, for the true meaning lies somewhere in the middle of the two views. There is indeed no rule of law, as we know it, yet there are many laws and there can be unhappy consequences for violating them. Many laws, no rule of law: investors are doing themselves a disservice if they do not come to grips with this paradox.

Still, law in the Russian Far East does not mean what it does, say in the United States. In the U.S., law is the glue that holds a deal together; signing a contract "seals" a deal. Law represents a set of (generally) neutral rules to which all parties must adhere, and provides penalties and enforcement mechanisms if they don't. In that sense, the law is the critical factor in every transaction, because it provides the context in which every business deal takes place.

There is no such law in the Russian Far East. This is not to say there is no law at all, but rather that the *significance* of law is different. Law is emphatically not an objective set of rules which applies equally to all parties and includes meaningful penalties and enforcement mechanisms. Law is not the essential backdrop against which transactions unfold, but is merely one of many factors that determine the fate of a venture. Indeed, ranking the elements that shape most deals in the Russian Far East, law takes a back seat to personal, political, culture and economic factors.

Ranking the elements that shape most deals in the Russian Far East, law takes a back seat to personal, political, cultural and economic factors.

There are three categories of Russian law, each of which has a different significance for those trying to conduct business in Russia: **Relationship Law**, **Bureaucratic Law**, and **Substantive Law**.

1. Relationship Law

Russia is not now and never has been a Western-style rule-of-law society. It is fundamentally a relationship society, where whom you know is more important than what the rules say, and where most rules are not really "rules" at all, but are rough guidelines for action, subject to endless variations when applied in practice. In this respect, Russia is closer to Japan, Korea and other Asian countries than to the West. The economic success of the Asian "relationship societies" is common knowledge. It suggests, first, that Russia need not necessarily adopt a rule-of-law model to succeed and, second, that Western investors in Russia would do well to learn from their experience (both good and bad) in Asia.

Russia's relationship society gives a specific meaning to the significance of law. One subset of Russian law consists of rules which are meaningful not as rules per se, but as tools for developing relationships: we will call these **relationship laws**. Large portions of Russian contract law and corporate law belong in this category.

Take contract law, for example. In the West, contract negotiations tend to focus on the substance of what is being negotiated because, in a rule-of-law society, the content of the contract, down to the smallest details, has considerable meaning. In Russia's relationship society, the significance of contract negotiations tends to lie in the negotiating process and the relationships that develop therein, rather than in the final result, the contract.

The *content* of the contract is significant, but since a foreign party's ability to enforce the contract is often dubious or cost-prohibitive, the real significance of the contract lies in the process of securing it, in the improved mutual understanding which can and should result from contract negotiations, and in the contract as a guideline and a statement of the parties' relationship and intent to work together to achieve a common goal.

In Russia's relationship society, the significance of contract negotiations tends to lie in the negotiating process and the relationships that develop therein, rather than in the final result, the contract.

The significance of most joint venture negotiations lies not in winning concessions to be included in the corporate papers, but in utilizing the negotiation of the corporate documents to ensure that the Russian and foreign parties are on the same wavelength about how their business will actually run. We call these types of laws "relationship laws."

2. Bureaucratic Law

Overlaid on, and intertwined with, Russia's relationship society is a vast bureaucracy. Russian bureaucracy pre-dates the Revolution, but reached a zenith under socialism. For seventy years, the bureaucracy spun the regulatory web which held Soviet society together and allowed the centralized planned economy to function. Now it pervades every aspect of life, especially economic life.

Bureaucracy in the Russian Far East differs little from bureaucracy elsewhere. Its primary mission in life is to regulate. And it does so with a vengeance, producing daily a numbing volume of "sub-legislative" or regulatory acts.

In the economic sphere, not only is the sheer volume of rule-making intimidating, but an expansive philosophy of regulation allows the state to dictate matters which elsewhere are considered a prerogative of the private sector.

This is the second category of Russian law, which we will call **bureaucratic law**. Bureaucratic law has a number of features which define its significance for the foreign investor. The first is its sheer volume and its capacity to show up everywhere. Second, since the regulations are produced by people with no experience (and generally no interest) in running a business, their logic (when such logic can be discerned) often contradicts sound business practice and runs counter to the reality of operating a business. Regulations typically place a premium on form over substance.

Bureaucracy in the Russian Far East differs little from bureaucracy elsewhere. Its primary mission in life is to regulate. And it does so with a vengeance...

Third, regulations are typically enforced arbitrarily, corruptly or not at all. When they are enforced, they often rely upon sanctions which don t really hurt that much. Fourth, regulations often contradict the law which they are supposed to implement and each other. Finally, it is hard to find out about regulations, especially on the local level, because, generally, they are not published in a consistent manner, nor are they widely available.

These features of bureaucratic law can make doing business in the Russian Far East very difficult. The foreign investor has a choice. He can divert resources from his business and expend them, instead, on an effort to know and comply with all applicable regulations, with no guarantee of success. Or, he can downplay the significance of compliance, risk that he has guessed wrong, and run afoul of the bureaucracy in a way that defeats his business purpose.

One approach to this dilemma is to saddle Russian partners or employees with the responsibility for complying with applicable regulations. That is sound insofar as it goes, though in reality the Russians themselves cannot ensure full compliance.

Another approach is to apply a cost-benefit analysis to specific regulations, weighing the risk of non-compliance against the cost of complying. A bewildering and hostile regulatory environment has forced many investors in the RFE to adopt this unfamiliar and uncomfortable approach.

3. Substantive Law

A third category of Russian law is derived from the fact that Russia is moving toward a rule-of-law society. Western-oriented Russian reformers have long viewed the rule of law as one of the principal features distinguishing successful market economies. A concerted effort to move Russia toward the rule of law was one of the early hallmarks of perestroika. Most reformers still view the development of a functioning legal system as an essential aspect of the transition to a market economy.

Over the last several years, that trend has moved from ideological debate to some degree of implementation with the passage of varied, significant and often well-crafted pieces of legislation. In the field of business, a basic legislative framework is now in place, covering such essential (and, in Russia, previously unknown or undeveloped) topics such as taxes, foreign investment, bankruptcy, secured interests, customs, property, and the like.

An investor can either try to comply with all applicable regulations (with no guarantee of success) or downplay compliance (and risk running afoul of the bureaucrats).

We will call some, by no means all, of these laws **substantive law** because they look and operate much like laws in a rule-of-law society. One feature of substantive law is that the laws are relatively clear, rational and available, subject to interpretation and application, not unlike legal norms in the United States. But to truly qualify as substantial law, these laws must be backed by enforcement mechanisms that work and sanctions that hurt. A violation of substantive law, in other words, has real consequences.

For now, laws which share both of these features are largely confined to those which generate revenue for the state: tax and customs law. The new Customs Code, for example, is a legislative achievement: understandable, internally consistent, and includes an emphasis on enforcement. In practice, too, sanctions for customs violations are effective; the customs service can impound disputed goods pending the results of an administrative appeal process.

Tax law is another field of increasing substance. It is not quite as clear, nor are its punishments as effective, as in the customs law. Russian authorities are striving to bring more substance to the tax area, to develop new rules, to refine old ones and to beef up their enforcement potential. The importance of a functioning tax system for Russian authorities at all levels of government is patently evident. Laws which generate revenue for the state are typically enforced and enforceable. They are substantive, deserve full attention, and are ignored at your peril.

Rule of law, of course, means more than passing new legislation. It means replacing legal nihilism with a culture of respect for the law, which cannot and will not occur in the foreseeable future. Yet rule of law is the trend, and already exists in limited areas.

A concerted effort to move Russia toward the rule of law was one of the early hallmarks of perestroika.

Conclusion

To sum up briefly, today's circumstances reflect a profoundly imperfect business environment. Attention to relationship law and substantive law generally contributes more to business success than does attention to bureaucratic law. However, a proper judgment can be made only on a case-by-case basis.

What we have said so far is that law matters in the "Wild East," but that it matters in a different way than it does in a rule-of-law society. The RFE is neither "lawless" like the old West nor "law-abiding" like the U.S. It is murkier than either of these views admits. It is a lawless society where law matters, a paradox with which investors must come to grips.

Kevin Block is the General Director of the Pacific Law Center in Vladivostok.

69 Turgenev Street
Khabarovsk 680000
Tel: (4212) 39-86-34
Fax: (4212) 39-86-35

2 Captain Shefner Street
Vladivostok 690001
Satellite tel: (509) 851-2470
Satellite fax: (504) 915-3144

The Pacific Law Center

A RUSSIAN-AMERICAN LAW FIRM

***

TAX AND CUSTOMS LAW
REAL ESTATE AND CONTRACT LAW
CORPORATE AND EMPLOYMENT LAW
BANKING AND CURRENCY LAW
PRIVATIZATION AND SECURITIES LAW

STRATEGIC PLANNING
DUE DILIGENCE INVESTIGATIONS
LOBBYING AND GOVERNMENT RELATIONS
POLITICAL AND BUSINESS RISK MANAGEMENT

***

Kevin Block, General Director
Nikolai Korolev, Deputy General Director

2 Captain Shefner Street
Vladivostok 690001
Local Tel: (4232) 22-47-84
Local Fax: (4232) 22-13-98

69 Turgenev Street
Khabarovsk 680000
Local Tel: (4212) 39-86-34
Local Fax: (4212) 39-86-35

Satellite Telephone: (011-7-509) 851-2470
Satellite Telefax: (011-7-504) 915-3144
Electronic Mail: plcenter@stv.iasnet.com

CHAPTER 11: TELECOMMUNICATIONS

- **Direct Dial Telephone and Fax**
- **Alternative Voice and Fax Networks**
- **Electronic Mail**
- **Telex**

Direct Dial Phone and Fax

Direct Dial

Direct dial using Russia's public telephone system usually means insufficient circuits, poor transmission, in a word: frustration. But, connections are more consistently happening on the first try, though there is still the chance of getting a busy signal repeatedly, or a recording that all lines are busy. All international carriers, such as AT&T, Sprint and MCI in the United States, and many public carriers in other countries now provide direct dial telephone service to major cities in the Russian Far East. (To reach smaller towns in the Russian Far East, it is still necessary to go through an international operator, who will enlist the help of an intermediary operator, either in Novosibirsk or Vladivostok.)

If you want to reach someone in the Russian Far East and you know the city code, dial 7 (for Russia) and then the town/city code (see examples below), followed by the phone number.

For direct dial, the city code plus the phone number should always make up ten digits. As a general rule, large cities in Russia have longer telephone numbers than do the smaller cities. For instance, Moscow and St. Petersburg phone numbers are seven digits with three-digit city codes for a total of 10 digits. Khabarovsk phone numbers, on the other hand, have six digits with a four-digit city code. Nakhodka and Sakhalin have five digit numbers with five-digit city codes. If you cannot get through yourself, an international operator can try the call for you at higher, operator-assisted rates.

Here are some Russian Far East city telephone codes for direct dial.

Blagoveshchensk	41 62 2
Khabarovsk	42 10 or 42 12
Magadan	41 30 0
Nakhodka	42 36 6
Petropavlovsk-Kamchatskii	41 52 2
Vladivostok	42 32
Yakutsk	41 12 2
Yuzhno-Sakhalinsk	42 42 2

Fax

Sending a fax to Russia using Russia's public telephone network obviously takes the same time and patience as telephoning. Although faxes can be sent by direct dial to certain cities in the Russian Far East, poor transmission can make faxes hard to read. Even if it appears that the fax has reached its destination, the sender cannot be sure that the receiver has a legible copy in hand.

Another problem: most fax machines in the Russian Far East do double duty as telephones and are not set on automatic receive. When you dial directly for a fax communication, it is best to use the handset and listen for the fax connection signal. If a person answers, inform the person that you want to send a fax. In Russian "Mo*zh-no pere-dat faks"* is the most direct way to ask. Usually the person on the other end will then activate the fax receive mode. You may get a communication error due to the switch and you may have to send the fax again. The telephone on the other end should, by that time, be set up to receive a fax.

Business centers in the Russian Far East open to public

Every Russian Far East city now has at least one business center where anyone can send and receive faxes, or make instant phone calls out of Russia. Some of these business centers are operated by private, international, telecommunications companies.

Dal Telecom has a business center in Petropavlovsk-Kamchatskii, **Nakhodka Telecom** in the Nakhodka Hotel and **Vostok-Infokosmos** at the Parus Business Center in Khabarovsk. **Sakhalin** and **Nakhodka Telecom** both offer phonecards for prepay international telephones. In Khabarovsk, you can walk into the Intourist Hotel, we are told, use the payphone in the lobby, dial 33 41 03, and the operator will connect you to the number you request abroad. Charge is US$4.50 to US$6.50 per minute and you pay at the hotel.

Every main post office has a business center where there is a fax sending and receiving station. These centers are convenient for occasional use (to send or to receive) if you do not need to send confidential material.

Alternative voice and fax networks operating in the Russian Far East.

Introduction

There is an alternative to direct dial using Russia's existing public access networks. Direct-dial connections to and from the Russian Far East are also possible via private, alternative access networks. These networks, called international overlay business networks (OBN), are private, subscriber-based, direct dial services and are now available in and from almost every area of the Russian Far East.

Delow we list some of the major OBNs operating in the Russian Far East. We indicate the identifying international access code for each of the companies, their service areas, their information number and their local office number. *These facts, of course, are subject to change.* All of the OBNs already do or plan to publish their subscriber directories.

DalTelecom. Joint venture between **Dalreo** and **Mid-Com Communications** (Seattle, Washington). Cities served include: Khabarovsk, Petropavlovsk-Kamchatskii, and Blagoveshchensk.

DalTelecom's numbers are accessed through Sprint (10333) and access codes start with (7) 509 01.

Local Office in Khabarovsk: 33 50 22

Information: (7) 509 01 60 0011

Information Fax: (7) 509 01 60 0002

Mid-Com in Seattle:

Tel: (206) 628-8383; fax: (206) 628-8769

Kriljon's U.S. representative is **Asian American Telecom** (AAT). Service area is Yuzhno-Sakhalinsk.

Kriljon's numbers are accessed through Sprint. Access codes start with (7) 509 95.

Local Office in Yuzhno-Sakhalinsk: 33 47 7

Information: (7) 509 95 1620

Information fax: (7) 509 95 1642

AAT offices in Anchorage: (907) 349-4933

Nakhodka Telecom. Joint venture with **Cable and Wireless** (Hong Kong). Service area includes Nakhodka, Vostochny and Vladivostok. Payphone service using pre-paid phone cards is available in hotels in Vladivostok and Nakhodka, and in many marine terminals and post offices.

Nakhodka Telecom's access codes start with: (7) 504 91.

Directory Assistance: (7) 504 91 5 1012

Local Office: 40 61 0/ 40 61 4

Information: (7) 504 91 5 1012

Information fax: (7) 504 91 5 1020

Sakhalin Telecom. Joint venture with **Cable and Wireless** (Hong Kong). Service area covers Yuzhno-Sakhalinsk, the airport and other areas on the island. Pre-pay phone-card telephones are available.

Sakhalin Telecom access codes start with: (7) 504 41.

Directory assistance: (7) 504 41 6 1011

Local Office: 2 24 49

Information: (7) 504 41 6 1020

Information fax: (7) 504 41 6 1029

Vostok-Infokosmos (VIC) is represented in the U.S. by **Asian American Telecom** (AAT). Service area is Khabarovskii Krai.

VIC's numbers are accessed through Sprint. (10333)

VIC's access codes start with (7) 509 31.

Local Office (Khabarovsk): tel /fax: 33 72 34

Information: (7) 509 31 32 29 99

Vostoktelecom is a three-way partnership with **KDD** and **Nissho-Iwai** (Japan) and **Interdaltelecom**. Service area includes Vladivostok, Nakhodka, Khabarovsk, Yuzhno-Sakhalinsk, Irkutsk and Yakutsk.

Vostoktelecom telephone numbers start with: (7) 509 85.

Some Local Offices:

Vladivostok: 22 85 30

Khabarovsk: 38 40 75

Yakutsk: 25 10 1

Information: (7) 509 85 1 2222

Information fax: (7) 509 85 1 2223

Often operators are not aware of the area codes for these OBNs. If you need to go through an operator (instead of direct dialing), don't let them discourage you. Just say the country code and the area code are correct and ask them to dial it. *Remember, some OBNs can only be accessed through specific international carriers and you may have to dial that carrier first.*

Electronic Mail

Your office is in Seattle; you have staff in Vladivostok. You've tried fax and telephone always frustrating unless you have "alternative access." You know about telex, but you want an alternative for sending text information quickly. Electronic mail (e-mail) is an efficient option.

What is e-mail?

At your personal computer, you correspond with others who, like you, are also receiving and sending mail messages via a personal computer. You write a message, you instruct your computer to send it to your correspondent's mailbox. Message delivery is practically instantaneous. When your correspondent at his or her computer looks into his or her mailbox, your message is waiting. E-mail is convenient. Messages are always clear, delivered exactly as you send them. You can send and receive messages at any time.

In the West, e-mail services are sold by many vendors. Western providers offer excellent customer service and will help you understand what hardware and software you need and help you open an account. E-mail correspondence to and from the Russian Far East is now commonplace for many firms. Here is some basic information about electronic mail.

Why is e-mail important?

It is clear, reliable, fast, and cost-effective. Users of e-mail are multiplying. E-mail is a major means of international business communications. There are many Russian organizations on e-mail network systems. These users can communicate through e-mail both within and outside of Russia.

What do I need to get set up?

Hardware, software, an account, and access to that account.

For hardware: a personal computer, a telephone line, and a modem which allows you to send data over the telephone line. For software: a communications program which instructs and permits computer-generated information to travel over the telephone lines.

How do I get an account on an e-mail system?

There are many e-mail systems operating: EasyLink, MCIMail, SprintNet are only a few. Accessing the larger e-mail systems from anywhere in the West is fairly straightforward. But from Russia and the Russian Far East, access isn't as easy.

Progress, however, has been substantial. Access to an e-mail system in the Russian Far East can be as simple as accessing it from your home office. That means direct, local, access. Direct access means a telephone call will connect you directly to the system on which you have a mailbox. Direct local access indicates that the telephone number is a local one.

The best scenario — in two parts.

(1) All your correspondents belong to the same e-mail system. That is, all have accounts or mailboxes on the same system network. If you know your correspondents and you have some control over the choices they make, this is the simplest form of e-mail communications.

(2) Your correspondents can access the e-mail network by way of a direct local phone call (an access node).

A second-best solution

In the absence of the perfect solution (e.g. a local direct dial telephone number (node) for the e-mail system to which you and most of your correspondents subscribe), there is a second-best solution.

Hook up to any available local node and learn the rigorous (but rewarding!) system of X.400 addresses, by which a correspondent can reach another on a different network with the correct X.400 address. Sending e-mail via X.400 addresses isn t easy, but it is worth the trouble.

X.400 Addressing

An X.400 address is the information necessary for users on different e-mail systems to communicate with each other through "gateways.." If you need to reach someone on a different network, you must have their correct X.400 address.

X.400 addresses have standard parameters, although these parameters are sometimes named differently. Call the help number of your e-mail network if you have difficulty using an X.400 address. They will help you determine how to set up the address correctly.

E-mail in Russian?

Yes, it can be done. The best way to send cyrillic text is via binary files. The original text is written in Russian, compressed to a binary file and sent via one of many common protocols (Kermit, Zmodem, or Ymodem.) The correspondent on the other end must decompress the file to be able to read it. (Computers on both ends must have cyrillic capabilities.) Networks provide help for sending binary files. For more information, contact your e-mail server.

Our X.400 e-mail addresses at *Russian Far East Update:*

To reach us at our **MCI** mailbox:

C=US
A=MCI
DDA: 386-6377
Surname: MILLER

To reach us at our **Sprint** mailbox:

C=US
A=Telemail
O=Mep.1
Surname=Miller
First name=Elisa

Telex...Respect it

Don't overlook the "workhorse" of communications

Although there are new ways to communicate with the Russian Far East (which we've discussed already), the old"tried and true" telex communications system is still worthy of use. First, it is quite reliable, easy to use, and provesa good back up if fax machines are out-of-order or phone lines are busy. Secondly, it is often still the only way to reach government offices in the Russian Far East, other than the telephone.

How to telex

You can ask someone to do it for you, a business service for example; or you can do it yourself. You will need a personal computer, modem and a subscription to any of the electronic mail services available in your country. Your electronic mail service should provide you with written instructions which will include telex instructions. Once you give your computer instructions to send a telex, not too much can go wrong as long as you have the correct telex number. You will need to enter the correct number and also add an "answerback" which is a series of letters which, for all the Russian Federation, ends in SU.

Those numbers with a PTB SU answerback represent the local public telex. These telexes are shared by different companies and institutions. When sending a message to a PTB SU answerback telex number, make sure that it is very clear to whom your message is directed, and, better yet, put their telephone number on it.

If a telex message doesn't go through and you are sure the number is correct, try again. Sometimes telex machines in the Russian Far East are down due to power shortages in the region.

Transliteration Guide

Telex messages, even in the Russian language, must use the Roman (Latin) alphabet. If you are sending a message in Russian, it must be transliterated using the Roman alphabet. Use the transliteration guide provided by Russia's Post Telephone and Telegraph (PTT).

You often ask

"Shall we send our messages in Russian or in English?" It all depends. If you have the capability to create your messages in good Russian, then Russian may get you quicker results because the document doesn't have to go to a translator at the other end. On the other hand, good English is much, much better than poor Russian. Good English is easy. Short sentences. Short words. Active voice. Lists are good. Also wise: identify the beginning and the end of your message.

Contact us about your telecommunications needs.

AmRussCom

Columbia Communications Corporation

Telecommunications for Russia's Sakhalin Island

The joint venture Kriljon is the leading provider of international telecommunications for Sakhalin Island's business community. Kriljon's team of professionals can provide your business with a complete range of products and services including:

- International Voice and Data Services
- C and Ku Band Satellite Systems
- Digital Switching Systems
- Mobile Radio Systems from Motorola and Midland
- Primary and Backup Power Systems
- Local Maintenance Staff

Let the experts at Kriljon handle all of your telecommunications needs on Sakhalin Island.

32 Communistichesky Avenue, Suite 642
Yuzhno-Sakhalinsk, Russia 693000
Phone (Sprint 10333): +7 50995-1620
Fax:+7 50995-1642
Local phone: 3-34-77

Russia Trade & Investment Services
Food –– Fisheries –– Forestry

INVITATION

Join the USDA–sponsored Food & Beverage Processing and Food Export Trade Mission to the Russian Far East.
September 11–24, 1994
Call 1–800–683–2455 or 202–331–7742.

William P. Mott
Agland Investment Services, Inc.
900 Larkspur Landing Circle #240
Larkspur, CA 94939
Tel: 415-461-5820
Fax: 415-461-6803

John V. Ward
Ward International
1745 N Street N.W. #200
Washington, DC 20036
Tel: 202-331-7742
Fax: 202-331-1719

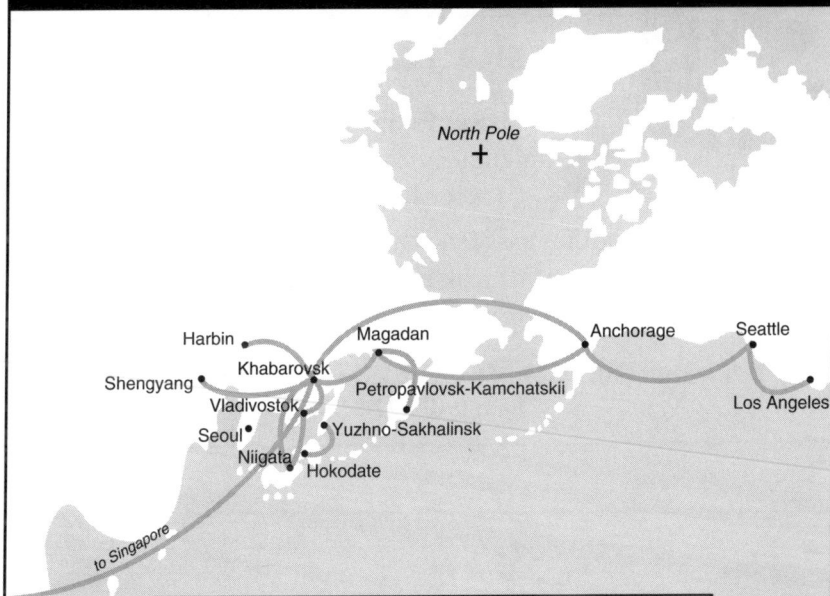

North Pole
+

Harbin
Shengyang
Khabarovsk
Magadan
Anchorage
Seattle
Vladivostok
Petropavlovsk-Kamchatskii
Los Angeles
Seoul
Yuzhno-Sakhalinsk
Niigata
Hokodate

to Singapore

Direct International Flights to the Russian Far East

from China
Harbin
Shengyan
Dalien
Chunchung

from Japan
Niigata
Amori
Toyama
Hokodate

from South Korea
Seoul
Pusan (charter)

from USA
Anchorage
Seattle

Major Airline Companies serving the Russian Far East:

Aeroflot
Alaska Airlines

Japan Airlines
Asiana

CHAPTER 13   HOTEL GUIDE

New hotel construction is evident in the Russian Far East. For instance, the Hyundai Company and the City of Vladivostok will open a 250-room hotel in downtown Vladivostok this year. Similarly, two new hotels (built with Chinese partners) will open in Nakhodka.

We should mention also that the historical Far East Hotel (Dalnii Vostok) in Khabarovsk will get a complete restoration before it reopens this year. Our list therefore below is already incomplete; that is the nature of the dynamic travel industry which exists in the Russian Far East. Our listings include a satellite telephone and fax number where possible, for easier communications.

Khabarovsk Hotels

Name: **Intourist Hotel**
Address: 2 Amurskii Boulevard
Local Telephone: 33-65-07
Satellite Phone: 7 (509 31) 42-22-20
Satellite Fax: 7 (509 31) 42-21-11

Name: **Business Center Parus**
Address: 5 Shevchenko Street
Local Telephone: 33-44-14
Local Fax: 33-72-70
Satellite Phone: 7 (503 31) 40-30-49
Comments: new, medium-sized.

Name: **Sapporo Hotel**
Address: 79 Komsomolskaia Street
Local Telephone: 33-27-02
Satellite Phone: 7 (509 31) 41-43-02
Satellite Fax: 7 (509 31) 41-40-88
Comments: primarily Japanese clientele.

Name: **Luidmilla Hotel**
Address: 33 Muravieva Amurskogo
Local Telephone: 38-86-65
Satellite Phone: 7 (509 01) 60-00-39
Comments: limited number of suites.

Name: **Hotel Amethyst**
Address: Corner of Lev Tolstoi and Kim Yu
                 Chen St.
Comments: new, spacious rooms; quiet
                 location; good security.

Yakutsk Hotels

Name: **Ontario Hotel**
Address: 20 minutes from downtown
Local Telephone: 6-50-58
Comments: built as traditional Yakutian log
                 building, western-style
                 (Canadian) accommodations.

Name: **Lena Hotel**
Address: 8 Lenin Prospect
Local Telephone: 4-48-90

Yuzhno-Sakhalinsk Hotels

Name: **Sakhalin Sapporo**
Address: 181 Lenin Street
Local Telephone: 3-66-29; 3-89-32
Satellite Phone: 7 (504 41) 6-25-50 or -20-05
Comments: mostly business clientele.

Name: **Santa Resort**
Address: Venskaia Street #3
Local Telephone: 5-91-74; 5-92-10; 5-92-74
Satellite Phone: 7 (509 85) 6-55-50 or -55-51
Satellite Fax: 7 (509 85) 6-55-55
Comments: Reservations Center: Tairiku
                 Travel Co., Ltd. 10th Mori
                 Building, 1 18 1 Toranomon
                 Minato-Ku Tokyo 105, Japan.
                 Phone in Japan: 03 3503 0660,
                 fax: 03 3503 7896.

Name:	**Hotel Lada** (formerly the Vostok)
Address:	154 Komsomolskaia Street
Local Telephone:	3-31-45; 3-18-45
Satellite Phone:	7 (504 41) 6-25-00

Name:	**"Address"** (Bed and Breakfast)
Address:	70 Pobedy Prospect
Local Telephone:	3-21-88
Satellite Phone:	7 (504 41) 6-22-26
Satellite Fax:	7 (504 41) 6-22-27

Name:	**Eurasia Hotel**
Address:	54 Vokzalknaia Street
Local Telephone:	27-44-66; 27-48-29
Satellite Fax:	7 (504 41) 6-20-03
Comments:	right on railway stations, nice Japanese bathrooms.

Name:	**Gorka I**
Address:	1B Kommunistichesky Prospect
Local Telephone:	3-55-45
Satellite Phone:	7 (504 41) 6-24-00
Satellite Fax:	7 (504 41) 6-20-04
Comments:	3 rooms, trying for high-level service.

Name:	**Gorka II** (Zagorodnaya)
Address:	right next door to Gorka I
Local Telephone:	3-89-30
Comments:	5 rooms, good for stately dinner; larger, older and more famous than Gorka.

Vladivostok Hotels

Name:	**Versailles** (Pronounced Versal)
Address:	10 Svetlanskaia Street
Local Telephone:	26-42-01
Satellite Phone:	7 (509 85) 1-51-51 or -51-54
Comments:	new hotel, also has a casino.

Name: **Vlad Motor Inn**
Address: Km 19 outside Vladivostok
Local Telephone: 21-58-29
Satellite Phone: 7 (509 85) 1-51-11 or -51-12
Comments: Canadian-style; reservations in
                   North America: (604) 787-1030.

Name: **Hotel Gavan**
Address: Krygina 3
Local Telephone: 21-95-73
Comments: new, located out of town; has
                   pool, gym, etc.

Name: **Acfes-Seiyo**
Address: 103 Stoletiia Vladivostoka
                   Prospect
Local Telephone: 31-87-60
Satellite Phone: 7 (509 85) 1 2115
Comments: new hotel.

Name: **Hotel Vladivostok**
Address: 10 Naberezhnaia Street
Local Telephone: 22-22-08 or 22-22-46

Vladivostok Restaurants

Name: **Nagasaki**
Address: 115 Svetlanskaia Street
Local Telephone: 26-50-43

Name: **Vladivostok Sakhura**
Address: In the basement of Hotel
                   Vladivostok
Local Telephone: 22-03-05

Name: **Moranbon**
Address: 6/25, Pervaia Morskaia Street
Comments: Korean cuisine

Name: **Versailles (Versal)**
Address: In the Versailles Hotel, 10
                   Svetlanskaia Street
Local Telephone: 26-42-01
Comments: American cuisine.

Name:	**Green Lantern**
Address:	Svetlanskaia Street
Comments:	Night club.

Name:	**Hingan**
Address:	2 Batareyna Street
Local Telephone:	25-37-11
Comments:	Chinese cuisine.

Nakhodka Hotels

Name:	**Nakhodka Hotel**
Address:	3 Shkolnaia Street
Satellite Phone:	7 (504 91) 5-21-19 or -21-21
Satellite Fax:	7 (504 91) 5-21-20

Name:	**Pyramid Hotel**
Address:	2 Vladivostokskaia Street
Local Telephone:	5-98-94 or 5-91-59
Satellite Phone:	7 (504 91) 5-22-09
Satellite Fax:	7 (504 91) 5-22-07
Comments:	operated by VIZIT Company.

Name:	**Hotel Dialog**
Satellite Phone:	7 (504 91) 5-21-82
Comments:	small guest house.

Note: this year two new hotels will open in Nakhodka.

Petropavlovsk-Kamchatskii Hotels

Name:	**Hotel Petropavlovsk**
Address:	Karl Marx Prospect
Local Telephone:	5-03-74 or 5-09-11
Satellite Phone:	7 (501 09) 64-00-44

Magadan Hotels

Name:	**Magadan Hotel**
Address:	8 Proletarskaia Street
Local Telephone:	2-10-14 or 2-59-86

Name: **Magadan Business Center and Hotel**
Address: 84 Proletarskaia Street
Local Telephone: 5-81-57
Local Fax: 5-82-23
Comments: JV partner is Adventures in Russia (Anchorage, Alaska), (907) 562-3000.

Blagoveshchensk Hotels

Name: **Hotel Druzhba**
Address: 1 Kuznechnaia Street
Local Telephone: 9-05-40, 9-03-93

Name: **Hotel Zeya**
Address: 8 Kalinin Street
Local Telephone: 2-11-00, 2-11-04

Name: **Hotel Yubileina**
Address: 108 Lenin Street
Local Telephone: 2-11-19, 9-38-96

SOME USEFUL ADDRESSES

1. Custom Houses (CHs) of the Russian Far East:

Yakutiia CH serves Yakutiia-Sakha Republic.
Address: 1 Chiryaeva Street.,
Yakutsk, Yakutiia-Sakha Republic
677000

Phone: 4-20-58, 4-00-13

Khabarovsk CH serves Khabarovsk krai except Nikolaevskii, Komsomolskii, Vaninskii, Sovetsko-Gavanskii, Ulchskii districts.
Address: Airport, Khabarovsk
680012

Phone: 37-14-82; Telex: 141195
DRAKON.

Vanino CH serves Nikolaevskii, Komsomolskii, Vaninskii, Sovetsko-Gavanskii, Ulchskii districts of Khabarovsk krai.
Address: Commercial Trade Port
Vanino, Khabarovsk krai.

There are 2 other CH: Amurskayya (in Komsomolsk-on-Amur) and in Birobidzhan (Jewish Autonomous Oblast).

Primorye regional CH serves all Primorye krai except Khasanskii district and some small ports on the eastern coast (See Nakhodka CH). Primorye CH does service Posyet settlement in Khasanskii district.
Address: Vladivostok, Custom
House 690000.

Nakhodka CH serves port settlements of the eastern coast of Primorye krai: Tikhookeanskii, Yuzhno-Morskoi, Livadya settlements and Partizansk town.
Address: Commercial Trade Port,
Nakhodka, Primorye krai, Custom
House 692900

Grodekovo CH serves Pogranichnyi district of Primorye krai.
Address: Grodekovo settlement,
Primorye krai, Custom House
690000

Khasan CH services Khasanskii district of Primorye krai, except Posyet settlement.
Address: Khasan settlement,
Primorye krai, Custom House
690000

Blagoveschensk CH serves Amur oblast.
Address: 1 Lazo, Blagoveschenshk,
Amur oblast   675000

Phone: 2-32-24

Petropavlovsk-Kamchatskii CH serves Kamchatka oblast.
Address: Sea Terminal,
Petropavlovsk-Kamchatskii,
Kamchatka oblast   683022

Magadan CH serves Magadan oblast.
Address: Commercial Trade Port,
Magadan oblast   685004

Sakhalin regional CH
Address: 56a Pogranichnaya Street.,
Yuzhno-Sakhalinsk, Sakhalin oblast
693000

Phone: 3-53-93; FAX: 3-53-93;

Teletype: 162084 ZALIV

Korsakov CH serves Korsakovskii, Dolinskii, Makarovskii, Poronaiskii, Noglikskii, Okhinskii, Smirnykhovskii, Tymovskii, Yuzhno-Kurilskii districts and Yuzhno-Sakhalinsk city of Sakhalin oblast.

Address: 2 Reidovyi Pereulok, Korsakov, Sakhalin oblast   694000

Kholmsk CH serves Kholmskii, Tomarinskii, Uglegorskii, Aleksandrov-Sakhalinskii districts of Sakhalin oblast.

Address: 69 Sovetskaia Street, Sea Terminal bldg., Kholmsk, Sakhalin oblast   694620

Phone: 2-23-14; Teletype: 152547 TEMP

2. Visa & Registration Departments (VRDs) of the Russian Far East:

Vladivostok VRD
Department of Internal Affairs
Vladivostok
Primorye krai   690000

Khabarovsk VRD
8 Ussuriiskii Blvd.
Khabarovsk   680000
Phone: 38-68-87

Komsomolsk-on-Amur VRD
Department of Internal Affairs
Komsomolsk-on-Amur,
Khabarovsk krai   681000
Phone: 4-03-62

Blagoveschensk VRD
18 50 Let Oktiabria
Blagoveschensk
Amur oblast   675000
Phone: 9-72-59, 2-67-83

Vladivostok VRD
Department of Internal Affairs
Vladivostok
Primorye krai   690000

Petropavlovsk-Kamchatskii VRD
Department of Internal Affairs
Petropavlovsk-Kamchatskii
Kamchatka oblast   683000

Magadan VRD
Department of Internal Affairs
Magadan
Magadan oblast   685000

3. Major airports of the Russian Far East:

Khabarovsk Airport
International Department
Airport, Khabarovsk
Phone: 37-32-42
Alaska Airlines: 378-804

Primorye Airport
Airport, Artem
Primorye krai
Phone: 3207
Alaska Airlines: 227-645

Magadan Airport
International Department
Airport, Magadan
Phone: 2-85-63, 2-76-55, 2-45-65

Alaska Airlines: 9-34-32

Sakhalin Airport
International Department
Airport, Yuzhno-Sakhalinsk
Phone: 3-32-25, 5-54-77

Blagoveschensk Airport
Airport, Blagoveschensk
Amur oblast

Petropavlovsk-Kamchatskii Airport
Airport, Petropavlovsk-Kamchatskii
Kamchatka oblast.

4. Foreign Consulates General (CG) in the Russian Far East

Japan CG (2 locations)
12 Mordovtseva Street, 5-63-60
Vladivostok, Primorskii krai
- and -
Hotel Sapporo, Khabarovsk

USA CG
22 Mordovtseva Street, Vladivostok
Primorskii krai   690000
Phone: 26-84-58; FAX: 26-84-45
US Business Center in Vladivostok
is located at the same address.

China CG
4 Amurskii Blvd., Suite 507,
Khabarovsk   680000
Phone: 39-90-07

Vietnam CG
41 Sportivnaia Street, Suite 34,
Nakhodka, Primorskii krai   692000
Phone: 2-65-37

India CG
14 Aleutskaia Street, Vladivostok,
Primorskii krai   690000
Phone: 22-96-69, 22-85-36,
22-81-10; FAX: 22-86-66.

South Korea CG
45 Aleutskaia Street, Vladivostok,
Primorskii krai   690000
Phone: 22-77-29, 22-77-65;
FAX: 229-9471.

Australian CG
17 Uborevicha Street, Vladivostok
Phone: 22-86-28.

North Korea CG
1 Vladivostokskaia Street,
Nakhodka, Primorye krai   692000
Phone: 5-52-10, 5-53-10.

5. Every Russian Far East territory has a Department for Foreign Economic Relations under the local Administration. One of the goals of this Department is to support activities of joint ventures on their territories. These Departments gather information for potential investors and often keep databanks on prices, foreign companies with representative offices, export & import data, "market surveys" as well as local rules and regulations on international trade and investments.

Yakutiia-Sakha Republic
Ministry of External Relations
11 Kirova Street,
Yakutsk 677022
Phone: 2-50-71
FAX: (095) 230-2919
Telex: 145126 LENA SU

Primorskii krai
22 Leninskaia Street,
Vladivostok 690110
Phone: (4232) 22-79-37, 22-10-19,
22-88-50
FAX: (4232) 22-52-77, 22-10-19
Telex: 152123 ECOM

Khabarovskii krai
19 Muraviev-Amursky Street,
Khabarovsk 680002
Phone: 33-41-87
FAX: 33-87-56
Telex: 141131 ASTRA SU

Amurskii oblast
135 Lenina Street,
Blagoveschensk 675023
Phone: 4-38-33, 4-36-52

Kamchatkskii oblast
1 Lenina Street,
Petropavlovsk-Kamchatskii
683000
Phone: 2-83-71, 2-51-08, 2-47-09
Telex: 244157 GERB SU

Magadanskii oblast
Administration of Magadan oblast

Sakhalinskii oblast
39 Kommunisticheskii Prospect,
Yuzhno-Sakhalinsk 693000
Phone: 3-49-08, 3-79-33, 3-55-68
Telex: 152123 AGAT SU

6. The Russian Far East also has 3 regional Chambers of Commerce & Industry (CHCI), non governmental organizations set up for foreign trade promotion.

Far Eastern CHCI
113 Shevronova Street
Khabarovsk 680000
Phone: 33-03-11, 33-11-30
FAX: 33-03-12
Telex: 141110 TEMP SU

Primorye CHCI
13a Okeanskii Prospekt
Vladivostok 690600
Phone: 5-97-30
FAX: 22-72-26
Telex: 213114 GLOBE SU

Yakutiia CHCI
15 Kirova Street
Yakutsk 677000
Phone: (84-11-22) 2-03-82, 6-01-24

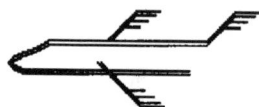

CHAPTER 15: CITY MAPS

This section contains street guides to the downtown areas of the two largest cities in the Russian Far East, Vladivostok and Khabarovsk. One distinguishing feature of post-Soviet city administrative activity is evident in these cities – street names are changing. The following are recent changes in Vladivostok:

Leninskaia Street is now Svetlanskaia Street

25th of October is now Aleutskaia Street

Kolkhoznaia Street is now Semyonovskaia Street

Dzerzhinskiy Street is now Fontannaia Street

For the latest information on street name changes in Russian Far Eat cities, we refer you to our monthly publication, *Russian Far East Update.*

The map of Khabarovsk first appeared in a special issue of *Russian Far East Magazine* (Anchorage, Alaska). This reprint appears with permission of the map's author, Don Croner.

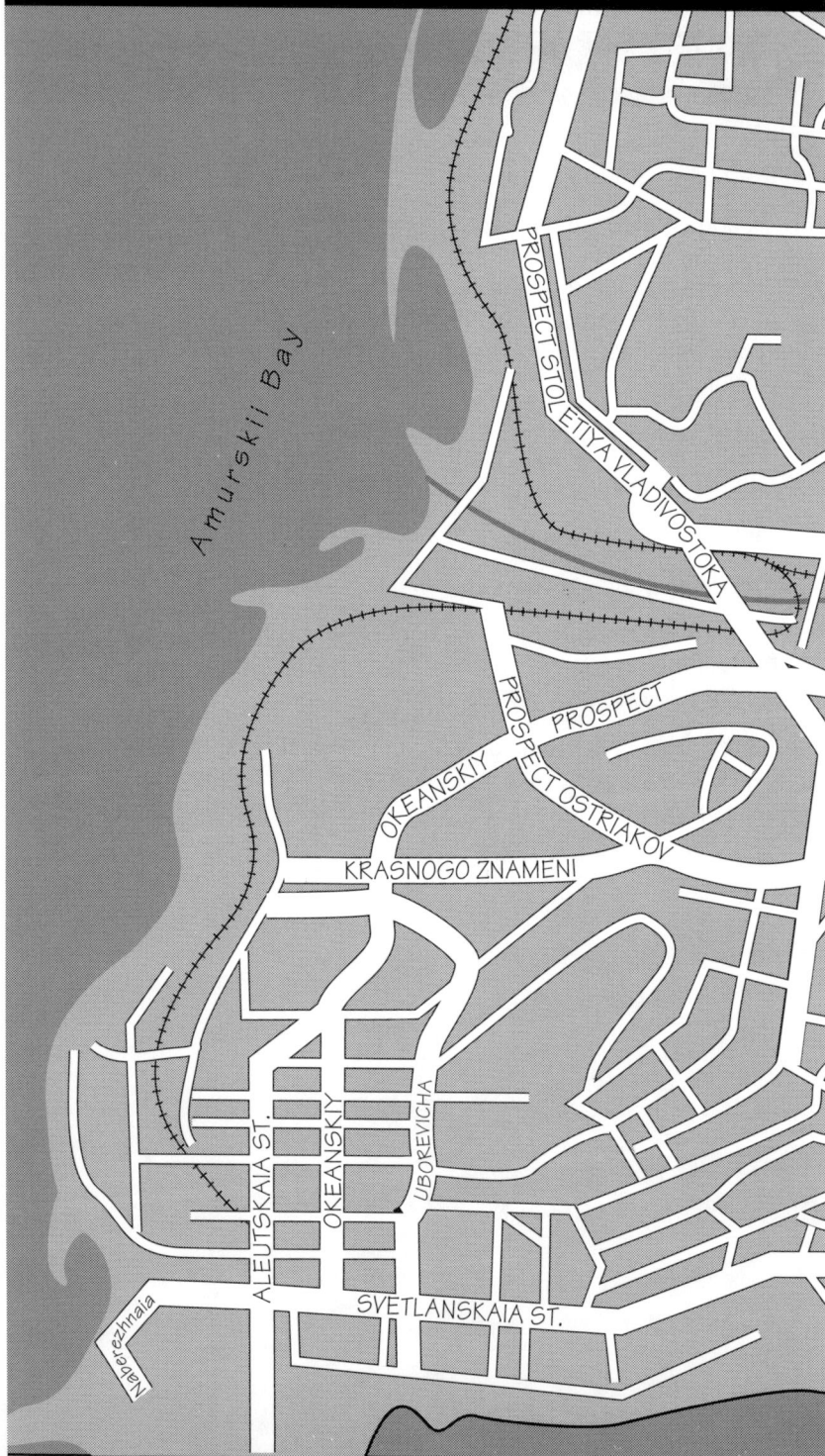

Amurskii Bay

PROSPECT STOLETIYA VLADIVOSTOKA

PROSPECT OKEANSKIY

PROSPECT OSTRIAKOV

PROSPECT

KRASNOGO ZNAMENI

ALEUTSKAIA ST.

OKEANSKIY

UBOREVICHA

SVETLANSKAIA ST.

Naberezhnaia

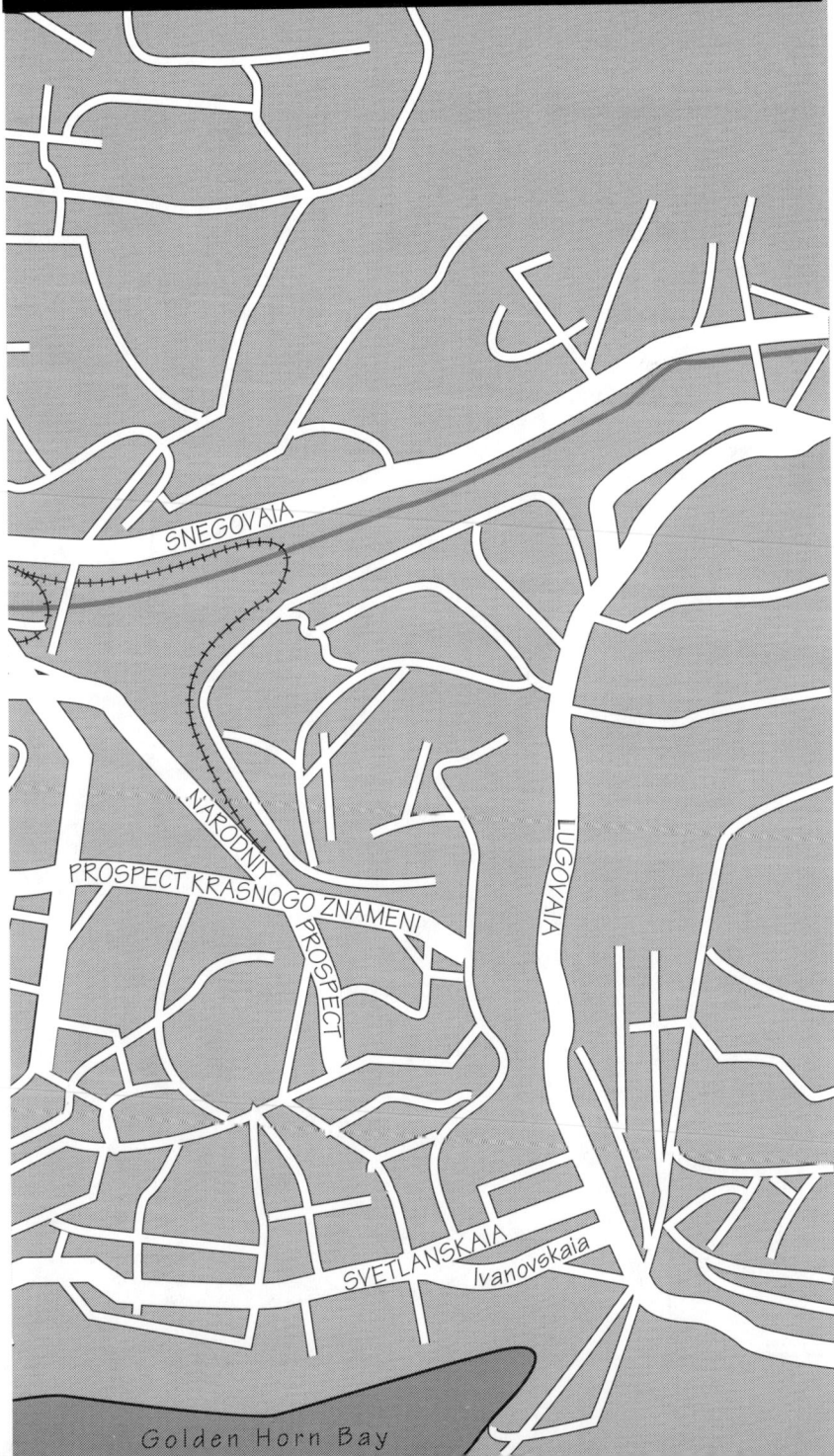

SNEGOVAIA

NARODNIY

PROSPECT KRASNOGO ZNAMENI

PROSPECT

LUGOVAIA

SVETLANSKAIA

Ivanovskaia

Golden Horn Bay

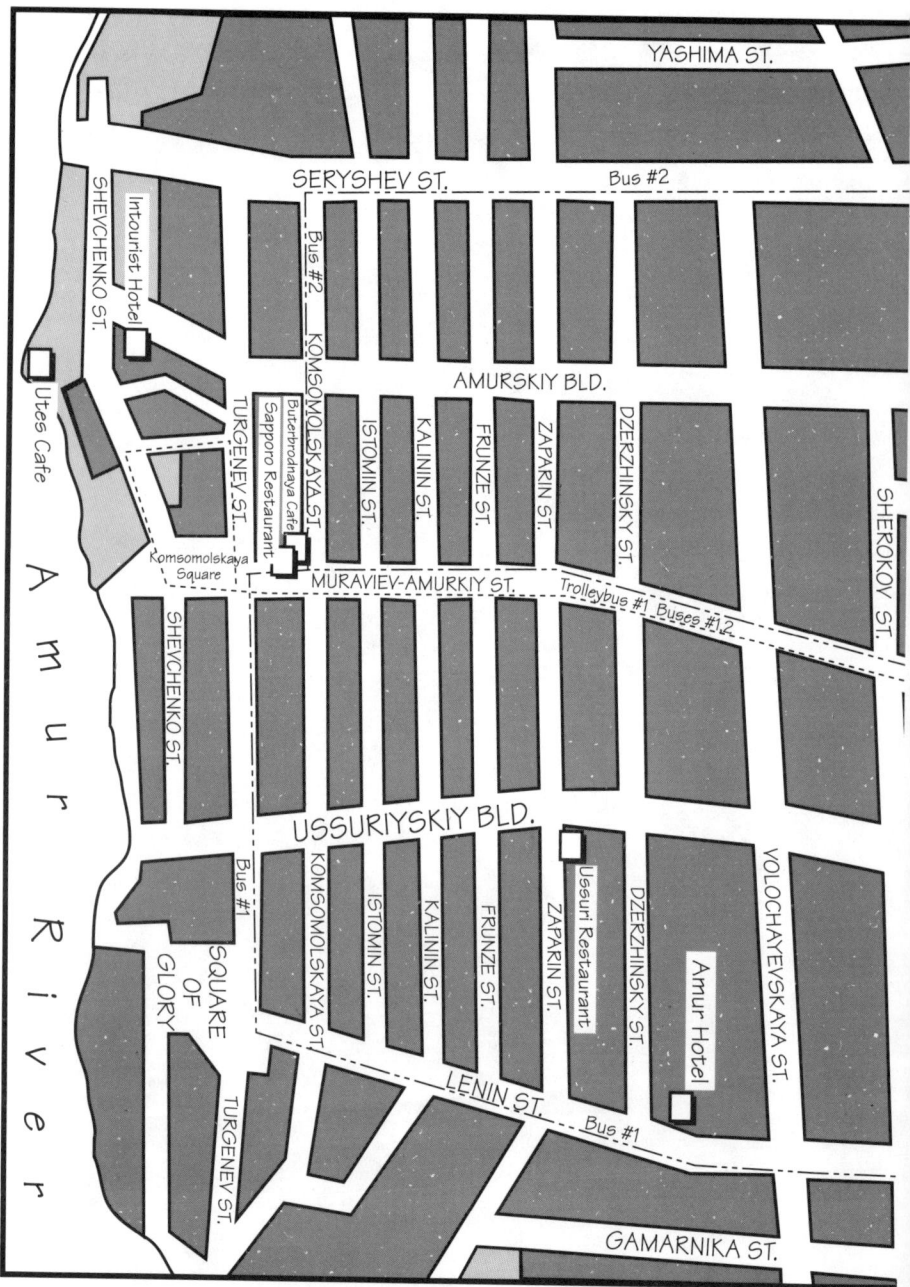

YASHIMA ST.

SERYSHEV ST.   Bus #2

SHEVCHENKO ST.

Intourist Hotel

Bus #2

Utes Cafe

AMURSKIY BLD.

TURGENEV ST.

KOMSOMOLSKAYA ST.

Sapporo Restaurant

Buterbrodnaya Cafe

ISTOMIN ST.

KALININ ST.

FRUNZE ST.

ZAPARIN ST.

DZERZHINSKY ST.

SHEROKOV ST.

Komsomolskaya Square

MURAVIEV-AMURKIY ST.   Trolleybus #1 Buses #1,2

SHEVCHENKO ST.

A m u r   R i v e r

USSURIYSKIY BLD.

Bus #1

KOMSOMOLSKAYA ST.

ISTOMIN ST.

KALININ ST.

FRUNZE ST.

ZAPARIN ST.

Ussuri Restaurant

DZERZHINSKY ST.

VOLOCHAYEVSKAYA ST.

Amur Hotel

SQUARE OF GLORY

TURGENEV ST.

LENIN ST.   Bus #1

GAMARNIKA ST.

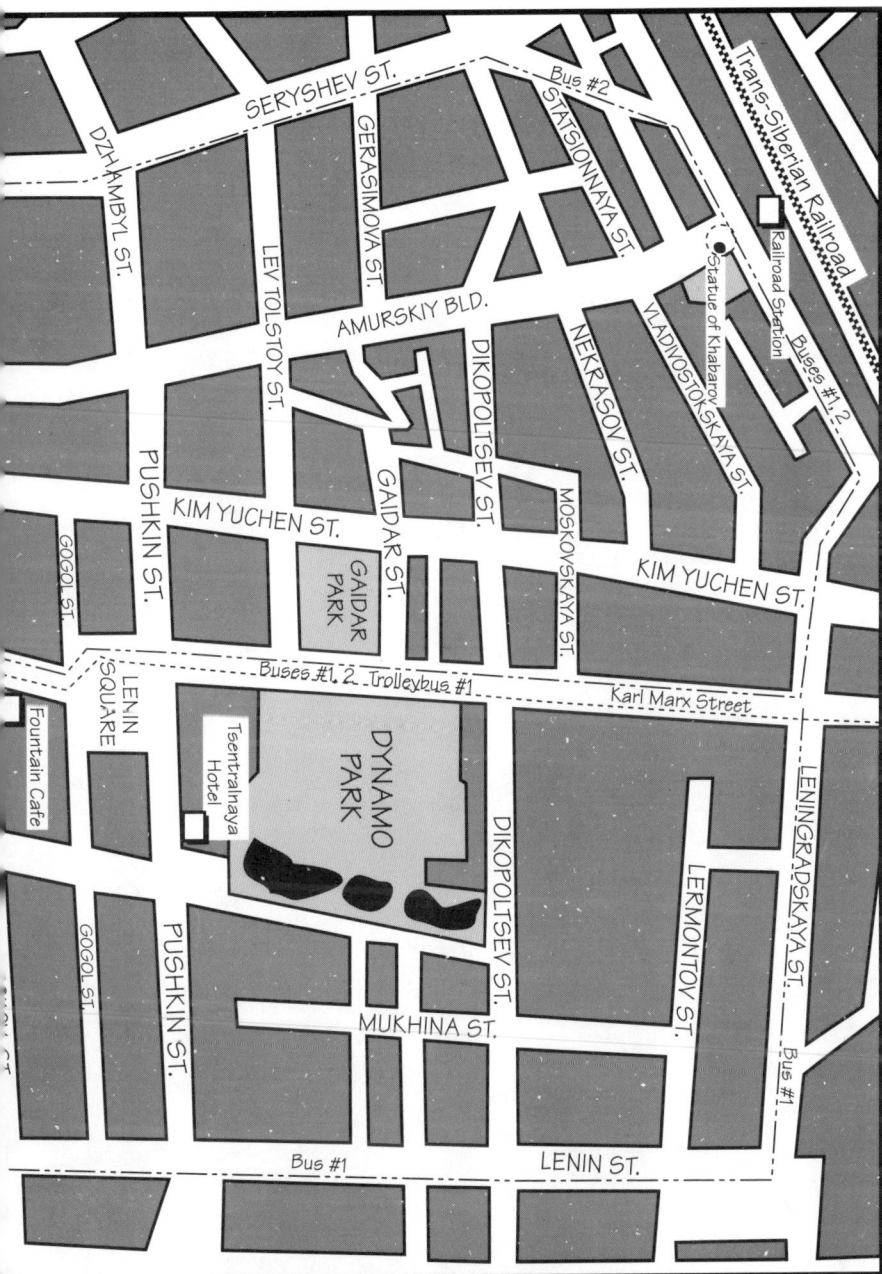

SERYSHEV ST.

Bus #2

Trans-Siberian Railroad

DZHAMBYL ST.

GERASIMOVA ST.

STATSIONNAYA ST.

Buses #1, 2

Railroad Station

Statue of Khabarov

AMURSKIY BLD.

LEV TOLSTOY ST.

VLADIVOSTOKSKAYA ST.

NEKRASOV ST.

DIKOPOLTSEV ST.

MOSKOVSKAYA ST.

PUSHKIN ST.

KIM YUCHEN ST.

GOGOL ST.

GAIDAR ST.

GAIDAR PARK

KIM YUCHEN ST.

Buses #1, 2, Trolleybus #1

Karl Marx Street

LENIN SQUARE

GOGOL ST.

Fountain Cafe

Tsentralnaya Hotel

DYNAMO PARK

DIKOPOLTSEV ST.

LERMONTOV ST.

LENINGRADSKAYA ST.

Bus #1

PUSHKIN ST.

MUKHINA ST.

Bus #1

LENIN ST.

CHAPTER 16: LIST OF ADVERTISERS

ABN/AMRO
Agland Investment Services, Inc.
Alaska Airlines
Alaska Tramper Service, Inc.
American President Lines Ltd.
AmRussCom
Archer Daniels Midland Company
ATIS America
Bering Air
CH2M HILL International Services
Commercial Pacific Business Center
Commonwealth Steel Co. Ltd.
Corporate Adviser Pty Ltd.
Dean & Lake Consulting, Inc.
Destination Development, Inc.
DHL Worldwide Express
Dimond Electric Co. Inc.
Forest-Consult
Foundation for Russian-American
    Economic Cooperation
Johnson & Higgins of Washington Inc.
The Jore Group of Companies
Lobana Co., Ltd.
Merit Steamship Agency Inc.
MMMMS Consortium
Mutual Travel

Nakhodka Telecom
Naodan Chartering Inc.
Pacific Law Center
Pacific Rim Telecommunications
Placer Dome Inc.
Regiobank
Rialto International Inc.
Royal Seafoods Inc.
Russia Far East/Asia Connection
Russia/Central Asia Travel Resources
Sakhalin Telecom
Samwhan Corporation
Sangdong Corporation
SAT Airlines
Sea-Land Service Inc.
SOVCAP Inc.
Stanford University Press
Sunmar Shipping, Inc.
Travco Industrial Housing, Ltd.
U.S. Bank
United Persons Incorporated
USR Express, Inc.
Vancouver Port Corporation
Vlad Motor Inn J.V.
Western Pioneer Shipping Services
World Class Products Ltd.

RUSSIAN FAR EAST
Update

A monthly newsletter in its fourth year of publication, the **Update** covers a variety of topics affecting business operations in the territories of Russia's Pacific Coast.

Russian Far East Update is the foremost intelligence source on "who's doing what" in the Russian Far East and reports on industry, trade, banking and finance, transportation, and local politics. The *Update* also provides readers with practical information: shipping, telecommunications, hotels, air routes.

Yes!

I'd like a one-year subscription (twelve issues) to **Russian Far East Update.** I understand that I may cancel at any time, and receive a full refund on any unmailed issues.

Name:	☐ US/Canada:	US $275
Firm:	☐ International:	US $335
Address:	☐ Russia Air Express:	US $375
	Washington residents please add 8.2% sales tax	
	Total	
Telephone:	☐ My check is enclosed.	
Fax:	☐ Please bill my Visa/MasterCard: Card #	
Russian Far East Update Post Office Box 22126 Seattle, Washington 98122 Tel: (206) 447-2668 Fax: (206) 628-0979	Exp. Date Signature	